Thriving

NOT SURVIVING

Thriving

NOT SURVIVING

THE 5 SECRET PATHWAYS TO HAPPINESS, SUCCESS, AND FULFILMENT

GINA GARDINER

Thrive
TOGETHER TRIBE

Hi Denise - Marie
Sorry its taken so long. Ingrams didnt
inform me the book was returned to them. I
look forward to speaking with you next month
Best wishes
Gina

6 Ardleigh Court, Ardleigh, Essex, CO7 7LA | 01206 230497 | 07833 183 327
georgina.gardiner@gmail.com | www.genuinely-you.com

GENUINELY YOU

Thriving Not Surviving

The 5 Secret Pathways to Happiness, Success, and Fulfilment

By: Gina Gardiner

#1 International Best Seller in
20 categories in 4 Countries

For More Information and
Book Bonuses Visit:
www.thrivetogethertribe.com

Thriving Not Surviving

The 5 Secret Portals To Happiness, Success and Fulfilment

LinkedIn: https://www.linkedin.com/in/ginagardinerassociates

Facebook: https://www.facebook.com/genuinelyyouprograms/

Facebook Group: https://www.facebook.com/groups/genuinelyyou/

Website: www.genuinely-you.com

Tribe Website: www.thrivetogethertribe.com

Email: info@genuinely-you.com

1st Edition 2017 Version 1.10

First Published in 2017 for Georgina Gardiner by Evolve Global Publishing

PO Box 327 Stanhope Gardens NSW 2768

info@evolveglobalpublishing.com www.evolveglobalpublishing.com

Book Layout: © 2017 Evolve Global Publishing

ISBN: 978-1-64136-361-7 (Paperback-Ingram)

ISBN: 978-1-64136-362-4 (Hardcover-Ingram)

ISBN-13: 978-1977855084 (Createspace)

ISBN-10: 1977855083 (Createspace)

ISBN: 9781370577286 (Smashwords)

ASIN: B074BPBLD3 (Amazon Kindle)

This book is available on Barnes & Noble, Kobo, Apple iBooks (digital), and Google Books (digital).

Table of Contents

Dedication xi

Acknowledgements xiii

About the Author xv

Introduction 1

Chapter 1– My Rocky Road to Happiness, Success, and Fulfilment 7

My Story 7

Your Biggest Fears Are Likely to Be Unfounded 14

We Are All Capable of So Much More 18

Chapter 2– The 7 Underpinning Principles 21

Principle 1–Permission 21

Principle 2–Perspective 23

Principle 3–Focus 27

Principle 4–Love 30

Principle 5–Forgiveness 31

Principle 6–Gratitude 36

Principle 7–Playfulness 38

Chapter 3– The 7 Connecting Themes 41

Connecting Theme 1–Mindfulness 41

Connecting Theme 2–The Survival Game 47

Connecting Theme 3–The Way to Lasting Change 49

Connecting Theme 4–The Power of Language 51

Connecting Theme 5–Taking Ownership 57

Connecting Theme 6–Strength and Vulnerability 61

Connecting Theme 7–Faith 65

Chapter 4– Secret Pathway 1–Belief 69

Beliefs Create Our Reality 69

How Beliefs Are Installed 70

Survival–Our First Priority 71

Our Beliefs Become Our Reality. What We Can Achieve Is Determined by Our Beliefs 71

If You Believe You Can't, You Won't. Believe You Can, and You Are Halfway There 72

Solving the Unsolvable 73

Prevalent Limiting Beliefs 74

Sadie 84

Jade 85

Peter 86

Keith 87

Chapter 5– Secret Pathway 2–Love 89

Secret Pathway 2–Love 89

You Are the Common Denominator 90

Every Relationship You Have with Others Is a Reflection of the Relationship You Have with Yourself 91

Your Relationship with Yourself 92

Our Beliefs about How Lovable We Are Have Enormous Power 93

Loving Yourself 94

Making Friends with Your Physical Self 95

Make the Most of Yourself Physically 96
Loving and Cherishing Your Body 98
Nourishing Your Body Is About So Much More Than Food 100
Looking After Yourself Emotionally 100
Dealing with Negative Emotions 101
Your Self-Care 103
Being Your Own Best Friend 104
If You Find It Difficult 107
Creating Loving Relationships with Others 107
Wanting to Change Your Partner 115
Being a Victim 116

Chapter 6– Secret Pathway 3–Success 119
Create and Share Your Clear Vision for Success 124
Ready? Then It's Action Time. Here's What to Do 127
Kiss the Frog 129
Your Expectations 131
Crossing the Line of Perturbation 134
Challenging Your Comfort Zone 136
Time 138
Energy 142
Money 148

Chapter 7 – Secret Pathway 4–Choice 155
Uncovering Choice in Times of Change and Transition 159
Need 1: Certainty 164
The Certainty-Uncertainty Paradox 167

Excellence 169
Need 2: Uncertainty or Variety 169
Need 3: Significance 170
Need 4: Love and Connection 172
Needs 5 & 6: Spiritual Needs of Growth and Contribution 173
Addiction and the 6 Needs 175
The Role of Choice in Life's Transitions 179
The Happiness Challenge–Why Not Choose to Try It? 180

Chapter 8– Secret Pathway 5–Purpose and Fulfilment 185
Material Wealth 190
Ego vs. Inner Wisdom 193
Are You Living Your Dream? 197
Challenge Yourself 199
We Are All One! Being of Service 200
Random Acts of Kindness 201
Gratitude 202
Faith 204

Chapter 9 - This Is Not The End 207

Dedication

I would like to dedicate this book to Jamie, my nephew who despite battling with a rare medical condition all his life has defied all the odds and has just reached the age of 41.

Acknowledgements

I would like to take this opportunity to thank everyone who has supported me over the years, particularly my sister Paulie and her husband Dave, Aunty Jill and my many, many friends who keep me going. My thanks and love to you all.

I am forever grateful to my clients for allowing me into their lives. It is a real privilege; one I appreciate hugely. Watching them step into their true power gives me great pleasure and satisfaction. I am incredibly humbled at the honour they give me by inviting me to be part of their journey.

A special thank you to John North who has provided exceptional support, encouragement and technical know-how in getting the book published and setting up the platform for Genuinely You and The Thrive Together Tribe, especially as my lack of technical ability has required much hand holding! My thanks to James and Nancy for their help too.

My ongoing thanks to my team particularly Sarah and Vicky who support me on a day to day basis – I couldn't do it without you!

About the Author

Gina Gardiner is a number one International best-selling Author, Motivational Speaker, Empowerment Coach, and Transformational Leadership Trainer, NLP Master Practitioner and Coach, with well over 30 years' experience in helping people achieve happiness and success.

She has supported many individuals and couples to develop a greater sense of self-worth and the confidence to challenge and change limiting beliefs in order to become more loving towards themselves and others. She is passionate about helping her clients to achieve their full potential–to become their genuine best selves.

Gina, herself, learned to walk twice as an adult whilst running an award-winning school, for the most part from a wheelchair. The gift of this experience was her development of a unique approach to life and leadership development. She left headship in 2004, and since then has worked with countless individuals and couples, helping them to learn the lessons from their past, in order to achieve happiness and fulfilment.

Gina believes that disability is a metaphor for life. She tells people:

> *If you believe that you lack the time, money, or expertise, or if you fear you are not good enough or pretty enough, or that you are too old, too young, too fat, too short, too poor, or too uneducated to achieve your dream, then chances are–you will fail.*
>
> *The difference between those who hold these limiting beliefs and my disability is that whilst those who have a deeply held belief, take that belief with them in everything they do, every second of every day, in every situation, I could choose to deal with my lack of mobility by wheeling away in my electric wheelchair. Thus, I allow my wheelchair to serve me,*

> *not limit me. Most people carry their limiting beliefs around with them into every situation and, as a result, live a life which is completely limited by those beliefs.*
>
> *Life can be incredibly challenging: relationships, work, finances, and health all vie for our attention. We are all pulled this way and that way, and there are times when it can feel overwhelming. The quality of our thinking makes an enormous difference to the quality of our lives. Being mindful and learning to focus on what you can do rather than what you can't, will significantly improve the quality of your life.*

Gina walks her talk–all the strategies she offers through her books and programmes are based on strategies she has used personally and with her many clients, who have achieved great success from using them. Her work is the culmination of personal experience and decades of working with people to help them achieve personal empowerment and fulfilment.

Gina has experienced incredible challenges and setbacks and understands just how difficult it is to pick yourself up and start again. Holding the space for her clients, listening not only to what they say, but to what is left unsaid, and giving them a safe environment where they feel heard and valued is a vital part of her work.

She has a wealth of experience in working with children and adults from all walks of life, and a real passion to make a positive difference. She cares deeply and has dedicated her life's work to empowering others.

Introduction

Reclaiming Your Self-Worth

If only I were smarter, then I would be happy.

If only I were prettier, then I would be satisfied.

If only I had more money, then I would be free from stress.

If only I were thinner, then I would be ready to chase that dream.

If only I were taller, then I would be more involved and outgoing.

Have you ever found yourself thinking along those lines?

Lack of self-worth is a modern-day epidemic. Because our need to belong, to be valued, and to be seen and heard by others–the most basic and ancient of human needs–are missing in many people's lives today, many of us are suffering from loneliness, depression, and a general feeling of malaise. This low self-worth and malaise have caused many of us to believe that something is missing from our lives. This, in turn, can lead us on an endless search for happiness, success, and fulfilment.

For some, the search can be as elusive as the search for the Holy Grail, and just as frustrating. Alcohol, food, drugs, sex, shopping, endless relationships which fall apart, hours and hours perusing the Internet, and working too long and too hard, are examples of common ways people conduct their search for fulfilment. While these excesses may give momentary satisfaction, they fail to provide a real solution.

As an empowerment coach, motivational speaker, and bestselling author, for nigh on forty years, I have had the opportunity to work with thousands of people from a wide variety of backgrounds, guiding them on their journeys to purpose and fulfilment. I have helped them to develop a greater sense of self-worth and the confidence to challenge and change limiting beliefs in order to become more loving towards themselves and others. I help each person to achieve their full potential–to become their genuine best self. And that's what I'm providing you within this book: step-by-step guidance so that you can achieve your full potential to become your genuine best self.

Thriving Not Surviving is designed to help you get the very best out of life. This life is not a rehearsal; it is the real deal. Each of us has to navigate the journey of our life; most try to manage without the benefit of maps, SAT NAVS, travel books, or personal guides. The result is that it is all too easy to find yourself stuck in a dreary environment where everything feels like a struggle.

Loneliness, frustration, stress, and anxiety, feeling unworthy or unloved, allowing past problems to limit the possibilities of the present and the future, lack of direction and purpose, failed relationships, unfulfilled dreams, feeling low and depressed, fearing failure or success are frequent every-day existences for many people.

Life offers lots of challenges, detours, and seeming dead ends. These can stop you in your tracks, causing you to get stuck in the morass of feeling overwhelmed, or they can act as the impetus to a better way of being. That is where *Thriving Not Surviving* can help you; it offers a SAT NAV, so you can achieve your deepest desires more easily. Plus, you'll read lots of examples of people just like you, that have used the principles and strategies to navigate their way through life's challenges.

It is important to remember that you remain in the driving seat. It is up to you how fast you go, where you begin your journey, and which elements you want to focus on.

Thriving Not Surviving contains three distinct interconnected sections. Together they provide all the principles, strategies, and tools for a truly happy, successful, and fulfilling life.

Section 1: The 7 Underpinning Principles

These 7 principles will provide the strong infrastructure you'll learn to develop, on which sit the **5 Secret Pathways** that we'll explore in the book's final section.

Here are those 7 foundations:

- Permission
- Perspective
- Focus
- Love
- Forgiveness
- Gratitude
- Playfulness

If any of these are missing, it is impossible to sustain ongoing success in any area of your life; so we're going to make sure you've established all 7 with solidity.

Section 2: The 7 Connecting Themes

These themes infiltrate the very fabric of our lives, yet most people have no idea of their power to help or hinder:

- Mindfulness
- The Survival Game
- The Way to Lasting Change (Unfamiliar/Familiar)
- The Power of Language
- Taking Ownership
- Strength and Vulnerability
- Having Faith

Section 3: The 5 Secret Pathways

Each of these 5 Secret Pathways offers you a different route on the journey to a happy, successful, and fulfilling life:

- Belief
- Love
- Success
- Choice
- Purpose and Fulfilment

Thriving Not Surviving gives you the opportunity to learn how you can journey along each of the 5 pathways with ease and grace, and so enhance the quality of your relationships, your choices, and your life.

Weaving is a metaphor for understanding life and how we fit into the world, our universe, and beyond. We know from archaeologists that the art of weaving has been carried out for over 20,000 years. To hold the threads of fabric together requires the taut structure of the warp thread entwined by the weft, which is built layer by layer revealing the patterns and design. In *Thriving Not Surviving*, the 7 Underpinning Principles act as the warp threads of the tapestry of life, the strong threads providing the strong base framework. The 7 Connecting Themes act as the weft threads; they wind through every aspect of your life. Most people are completely unaware of their power in working with both their warp and weft threads. The 5 Secret Pathways explore life's greatest challenges, adding colour, texture, design, and images to each of our tapestries. Individually each underpinning principle, connecting theme, and secret pathway offers a powerful tool to enrich and enhance the quality of your life; collectively they are positively transformational.

Even the spaces between the fibres have significance. When we experience a lack, a loss, where there is a hole in the fabric of our lives, we have the opportunity to learn and grow, to develop wisdom, resilience, and persistence. Just like the fabric takes on strength from the spaces, the gaps give us the opportunity to take a step back, to take stock and see things differently. *Thriving Not Surviving* offers you the opportunity to do just that.

It is important to recognise that engaging with all the components together, that is, the principles, themes, and pathways will give you the very best chance to achieve lasting happiness, success, and fulfilment. Embracing one or two of the components will make a positive difference, but just as many threads come together, to make a beautiful and rich tapestry, the principles, themes and pathways combine to thoroughly enrich your life and deepen your experiences, perspectives, and attitudes in the most empowering and beneficial of ways.

It is entirely up to you how happy, successful, and fulfilling your life will be. However, most people are completely unaware of the powerful impact they make, through their daily patterns of thought, speech, and action, on their own lives and on the lives of others. Furthermore, because people have no awareness of their own significance, they are powerless to change those aspects which are having a negative impact on the quality of their lives.

Thriving Not Surviving presents the principles and strategies that I have learned through my personal experience and the lessons I have learned from my clients, from other well-respected and erudite self-help leaders and through studying a variety of highly successful people and undertaking a great deal of research. All of the principles and strategies I present to you have been tried, tested, and proven to work. You will find you can readily incorporate the book's exercises and activities into your daily life.

Thriving Not Surviving provides the knowledge to help you identify where changes will help you create an even better quality of life for yourself and the people you care about, and you'll receive strategies to implement and sustain those changes.

In It–Together! Your Place in the Thrive Together Tribe

If you want the kind of lasting transformation we're exploring in this book, it is important to have someone in your corner to help you: witnessing your intentions, providing the right sort of support, holding you accountable, and celebrating your successes with you. Because the impact of having such a support group is instrumental in helping create and maintain a lasting change. I created just such a support group called the Thrive Together

Tribe. It is an online membership group, which offers a positive peer group, ongoing support, access to a bank of further information, and strategies to help you on your journey. Being part of the Thrive Together Tribe means you will have a huge body of supporters who believe in the power of YOU even when you are struggling to believe it yourself.

Being seen, heard, and validated are central pillars of the Thrive Together Tribe. There will always be someone on hand to offer a listening ear, support, and advice, or to simply hold the space for you. The Thrive Together Tribe will help you maintain your focus, so you can achieve your goals. It provides an opportunity to communicate with others who are going through the same challenges as you and those who have successfully moved beyond them.

Thrive Together Tribe members are grappling with the very big-life issues, hopes, and goals that we explore in *Thriving Not Surviving* because living their most fulfilled life as their genuine best self is the aim of the tribe.

Please go to www.thrivetogethertribe.com to learn more about the Thrive Together Tribe and to join us. We're holding a spot for you!

I'll be referencing the Thrive Together Tribe regularly throughout the book to remind you of this supportive community that invites you to join. Now, let's proceed on our *Thriving Not Surviving* journey, so you can take your first big step toward developing a greater sense of self-worth and confidence.

In chapter 1, I share a little of my own journey, so you can appreciate that I have had plenty of opportunities to put these principles to the test. I know from personal experience that incorporating the 7 Underpinning Principles, being mindful of the 7 Interconnecting Themes, and using the strategies within the 5 Secret Pathways has not only changed my life hugely for the better but also that of the many clients I've worked with. I hope it will do the same for you.

Chapter 1

My Rocky Road to Happiness, Success, and Fulfilment

My Story

You may say, 'It's all right for you, you haven't got my problems', and of course that's true, but I have faced my own demons and challenges and emerged stronger as a result of the battles along the way.

I know from my own story and from working with thousands of people that the one quality which makes the difference between success or failure, in pretty much every aspect of life, is self-belief. Unless you actually develop a positive belief in yourself and your capacity to change and grow, you will stay stuck in the same old rut.

The good news is that it is completely and utterly possible to develop a strong sense of self-belief where previously you had none. I know, because I have positive proofs from my own experience. I developed approaches and strategies that worked! They worked quickly, and the results have been great and long-lasting. The gift of my struggle was learning a unique approach to life and leadership, which I've since used with countless others to help them reach great success.

Over the years, I have refined my approaches through working with many clients, who come from all walks of life and who have faced a variety of challenges along the way. My clients and I have emerged on the other side feeling confident, powerful, and in control of our own destinies.

Abuse, brutality, calamity, death of a loved one, divorce, enmity, fear–I could go through the alphabet and list any number of significant challenges that my clients had experienced before we started working together. What my clients all had in common was the will to change. That change was achieved through their development of a great sense of self-belief.

Using the insights, approaches, and strategies that I'm going to share with you, clients just like you created new patterns of beliefs and behaviours that have, in turn, underpinned their ongoing and enduring happiness, success, and fulfilment. They changed their thought process, strengthened their emotional resilience, and developed a can-do mentality, to regain and maintain control of their lives.

Let me share a bit of my story, so you'll see where I'm coming from and what I mean.

When I left college, I became a teacher. I absolutely loved it, and for the first time in my life, I began to feel as if I belonged. I enjoyed early promotions, and at the age of 28, I applied for the deputy headship (vice-principal) of a large primary school in Romford, a very mixed urban area on the outskirts of London. When I went to visit the school to decide if I wanted to interview for the position, I was told by the head, 'I'm not really interested in you because we want to appoint a man'. (Things were far less PC in those days!)

I thought about what he'd said but decided to apply anyway.

On the day of my interview, the head told me that if there would be a male candidate with similar abilities as mine at the interview, he would get the job.

My interview went well, but bearing in mind what had been said to me before hand, I was shocked that I got the job. Once appointed, I discovered that the acting head, a female, had been told not to apply because they were going to appoint a man. Upon meeting me, she was not a happy bunny. Additionally, I was the youngest bar two on the staff. I was told that I'd been appointed to be the catalyst for change and that the staff were very reluctant to move from their old ways. I had a challenge on my hands!

Getting people on my side started with my proving to them that I was good at my job. Creating positive relationships and a shared understanding of the desired outcome, were to be vital components for success. The first term and a half were taken up with creating a vision for change and planning how we were going to achieve it. When the February half-term holiday arrived, I was more than ready for the break!

February 19, 1983–I was off skiing. The sun was shining in an amazingly blue sky. Majestic snow-covered mountains surrounded me as I sat on the chairlift, which rose above St. Anton in Austria.

The day before, I had made a spectacular 'bindings check' (meaning: a fall, to the uninitiated). All week, I had wrestled with the new pair of skis I'd been given for Christmas. They were 10 cm longer than those I had been used to. It had been quite a challenge keeping up with the other skiers in the party. I had fallen some distance, and I was shaken and bruised and extremely cross that had I torn my posh new ski suit from thigh to ankle.

It was Friday, the last day of our holiday. I'd decided to spend the morning skiing at the back of St. Anton where there was a lovely, gentle run, which went on for miles. The others wanted to go off and ski somewhere far more challenging. We agreed to meet at a favourite restaurant for lunch. In the meantime, I had a relaxed morning, skiing in beautiful surroundings, enjoying the sunshine, and practising my ski technique.

Lunch was great. I'd worked up a real appetite, and the banter was fast and funny. My friends were really enthusiastic about a fabulous run they had discovered that morning. They suggested I join them that afternoon; they wanted to ski it one last time before leaving for home the next morning. It sounded like fun.

We sat on the chairlift, admiring the spectacular views around us. Huge rugged mountains, deep purple monoliths, covered in sparkling white snow filled the horizon. The snow was so dazzling that it hurt my eyes, even through my sunglasses. The air was crystal clear, and I could hear the faint sound of bells from a church in the distance. I could smell the freshness and the scent of pine in the air.

Everything seemed brighter and clearer than in my real life back in Romford. There was a wonderful sense of timelessness as we seemed to float above the world below. Every now and then, I caught a glimpse of a brightly-clothed skier in the distance, and occasionally I could hear the "shhhhh" of skis on powder snow.

Approaching the lift station, all I could see was a gentle slope leading away from the chairlift. Two at a time we readied ourselves for the jump, edging forward on the seat and then pushing ourselves away before the seats disappeared into the shed in front of us.

We skied down the gentle slope and rounded a corner. There was before us a stomach-churning, dramatic drop into the valley far below. The descent looked steep, significant, and absolutely terrifying.

Little did I know that my life was never to be the same again . . .

Before now, I'd tackled black runs before. In themselves, they were no problem. I took a moment to steady myself. Everyone was quiet. Too quiet! It didn't take a rocket scientist to realise that this wasn't the slope they were expecting.

On one side, the world looked just as it had been from the lift, stunningly beautiful and incredibly vast, but on the other side, I could see a HUGE steep mogul field, descending several hundred feet to St. Anton in the distance far below. Through squinted eyes, I could only make out the tiny specks of cars on the road, way below.

The moguls on the first part of the descent looked as if some alien force had created them. They were over five feet high, and the slope was full of them. There were no obvious paths down, and at the far edge on either side, I could only see virginal powder snow.

Looking back, I saw that the slope now masked the ski lift; I knew there was no way back. I had watched the chairlift seats in front of me tip upside down for their descent down the mountain.

No one spoke. We stood for a moment, each lost in our own private thoughts. I felt sick. I realised the only way down was to ski. I took a huge breath and began my descent.

I slowly negotiated each mogul with care, concentrating hard on the small distance right in front of me and studiously avoiding looking down. Bit by bit I made my way down. The first couple of hundred feet were behind me. I began to breathe more easily. 'Maybe everything will be fine after all', I told myself.

I relaxed too soon and found myself in a very tricky bit. I kept skiing across the mountain looking for a safe place to turn. My mouth was dry, and my stomach was doing the loop de loop. I'd left it too long trying to find a better line when suddenly I lost a ski in the deep powder snow. I found myself falling. Down I went. I landed with a huge thump! I looked up to see a ski sticking out of the powder some thirty feet above.

I climbed painstakingly to retrieve it, and some twenty sweaty minutes later I had managed to climb up and reach it.

I started again. The going was a little easier, and finally, I joined my friends.

Each of us sat on our own mogul, like elves on toadstools. The moguls were about six feet higher than the surrounding snow, and there was very little space between them.

I could feel the sun was incredibly warm, and as we sat there, we could see the ice melting in the warmth.

Suddenly I found myself falling–the top of my mogul had given way. The more I tried to stop myself, the more I rotated. I tumbled down and down. I was bouncing from one mogul to another. The ice was hard as I banged from one mogul to another. My breath was knocked out of me as I fell and landed, slipped, and fell again. In the distance, I could hear a piercing scream and then blackness.

I became aware of light and then a terrible pain in my head. I tried to work out where I was. I lay dazed and disoriented. I remember feeling somehow outside myself.

I have no idea how long I lay there. In a strange way, it felt as if I was watching myself from a distance. Time stood still and so did my mind.

After some time had passed, my friends arrived. Anxious faces surrounded me. Their relief that I was still alive was palpable. With their help, I managed to sit up. I felt as if I had been run over by a steamroller.

They wanted to call for the blood wagon, and I was just as determined that they wouldn't. We were due to travel home the next day, and it was school on Monday, so I pulled myself together. I felt very strange at first, not quite there, but I somehow managed to ski very slowly down the slope, back to the hotel. The ski down took hours as every movement hurt, and I felt quite sick and dizzy.

I couldn't face food, and the night seemed endless as I kept reliving the fall. I had the mother of all headaches, and the room had a very annoying way of spinning around.

Morning finally arrived. We were due to travel home, and I couldn't quite get my act together. My friends had to pack for me, they took charge of my case and skis. I concentrated on getting myself dressed and getting onto the coach.

It was a hellish journey. Everything hurt. I felt as if I'd been run over by a tank. The flight was delayed, and I felt absolutely dreadful. We seemed to be on the move forever, but even the worst journeys come to an end; eventually, we arrived home.

At the time, I lived with my parents and after one look, my mum carted me off to the nearest accident and emergency department. I was told I had a concussion and a trapped nerve in my neck. I was given some painkillers, advised to take things easy, and then sent home.

Monday morning dawned. There was much to do that term to implement the plans for change. I struggled into school, all the while feeling rather strange. An hour later I was sent home, apparently not making much sense (but of course there were those on the staff who would say that that was fairly normal!). I tried again on the Tuesday and Wednesday and failed, but by the following Monday, I was back.

Four weeks later I was the deputy leader of a Borough ski party with 150 excited children. We were going to Switzerland. As the week progressed, I felt more like Quasimodo, but I was keen to pull my weight, so I pushed on and kept going.

Our last day of skiing dawned with thick mist. It was the children's medal day, so I spent the whole day acting as the race starter at the top of the mountain–It was really a struggle! By the time the last child had skied down through the slalom poles, I had nothing left to give.

After we all returned to the hotel, I made sure the children were OK before going to lie on my bunk–the top one! I considered how I was going to make it up the ladder. It now seemed incredibly high. I felt a huge sense of relief when I reached my bed. However, not for long! I suddenly discovered that I couldn't move my right side at all. I felt a moment of blind panic–I desperately wanted to go to the loo, but I couldn't move.

I prayed for someone to come, but I didn't want to shout and frighten the children. I thought 'What the hell is going on? What's happening to me?' Every moment felt like a lifetime. Just imagine for a moment how it would feel to be lying on a top bunk in a foreign country and suddenly find the right side of your body totally paralysed. Regardless of how much my brain was willing, I couldn't move a muscle!

Eventually, a colleague came to check on me . . . and then all hell broke loose. I was taken to a local hospital and transferred to Geneva University Hospital the next morning. Everyone else travelled home.

I felt very alone. All I had with me was a small bag packed hurriedly by a colleague. I managed to open the bag only to find three novels, a toothbrush, and no knickers. I'd not realised before, how important to my sense of security my nether garments were to me.

Some days later, after a battery of tests, I was flown home to my local hospital. After two weeks, as an inpatient, I was discharged. I had regained some movement and power, but things were far from normal.

May saw my return to school, but all I could manage was school and sleep. I was so pleased to make it to the end of the summer term. I was exhausted! Six weeks off school, I hoped, was going to give me time to recover and overcome the fatigue.

On August 8th that year, I received a phone call very early in the morning to say that John Hughes, my head teacher, had died in his sleep. The holiday proved to be anything but restful as I was immediately promoted to the acting head. The autumn term began, and I had to put my own problems aside, in order to deal with everything at school.

After a period of being the acting head, I was appointed as the permanent head–the youngest head in the authority. I was very green but determined the school should do well.

Little did I know that the school and I were to face many significant changes over the coming years.

My health continued to be a real struggle. Over the next few years, I was in and out of hospital undergoing one investigation after another as they tried to identify and treat the problem. Little by little, I was becoming more physically limited. By 1987, my mobility was so poor, I needed to use a wheelchair. I resisted–BIG TIME!

Your Biggest Fears Are Likely to Be Unfounded

I was worried about what others would think.

It was, by now, the summer holidays of 1987. Some friends and I went to visit the famous Wisley Gardens. I struggled to walk from the car to the ticket kiosk where there was a wheelchair for hire. I got no further. Rather than use the wheelchair I chose to walk, but because the fatigue was so bad, I only made it to the edge of the car park. There, I sat and waited two hours for the others to return. I did a great deal of soul-searching that day. I realised I was cutting off my nose to spite my face. As it was, soon after this, my hand was forced: Following a four-month stay in hospital, I had no choice but to use a wheelchair.

I was worried. I believed that the children, parents, and staff would think less of me if I used a wheelchair. I was frightened they would think that I couldn't run the school effectively.

What a waste of time and worry! The children at school didn't bat an eyelid, the parents were fine, and the local authority, nothing but helpful. All the sleepless nights and anguish were completely unnecessary. I was, in fact, less disabled at school at school than I was at home. This became even more evident after two bouts of failed back surgery in 1996 and 1998 when I became completely wheelchair bound.

I discovered that since I could use my brain, my hands, and my mouth, I could run my school very effectively. I'd learned a very important lesson: When something is entirely out of our control, we still have the absolute choice as to how we deal with it.

I could become a victim of my circumstances, moan, and bore the pants off everyone else, or get on with life, be useful, and enjoy it. The choice was a no-brainer for me. I'm sure many of you can think of a situation you have faced which has appeared to be out of your control. Remember that, however bad it may seem, you always have the choice about how you deal with it.

To help me at school I bought a whiz-bang wheelchair that could rise to standing height. On the first day of using it, I came into assembly. I told a story about an incredible wizard. As he magically rose to become taller and taller, the chair rose too, and the children were mesmerised . . . until I found myself stuck at the top of a six-foot pole, unable to get down.

My health continued to deteriorate. Every medical intervention appeared to make things worse. Despite all the challenges, I was determined that school and the people in it should not suffer because of my physical limitations.

Towards the end of the summer term in 1996, I sneezed whilst in the garden. I felt something ping in my back. Over the next two weeks, things deteriorated significantly, and I was admitted to the hospital on the first day of the school holidays. Eventually, I was scanned and rushed into theatre with a ruptured disk. When I woke up, there were complications, making it impossible for me to put my left foot to the floor without fainting, because of the pain. I returned to school in September at the start of the term.

It took me until the Easter of 1998, with lots of nerve blocks, and a great deal of determination (my mum called it 'bloody-mindedness!') to walk the 80 feet to the bottom of the garden.

A few weeks later, the term ended for the summer. I was feeling exhausted but happy that the school was doing so well. I joined the staff for a celebratory meal that evening, but by the time I got home I was feeling rather unwell.

I was sick, and as I got up, I felt something ping in my back. Excruciating pain told me that I had done something significant. I was rushed to hospital and then into theatre. I'd ruptured another disk in my back.

Yet again, there were complications which left me unable to stand or walk at all. I was once again completely wheelchair bound. It was a real blow, but I was as determined as ever to run my school. One thing was of paramount importance: There must be no negative impact on my staff or the quality of education for my pupils.

You get what you focus on in life. If you focus on what you can't do, what is lacking and wrong, you'll feel depressed and disempowered. Sometimes you may find yourself in a situation where everyone else is focused on what you can't do, which means you must recognize the belief inside yourself, that you can do it, no matter what others may think.

I've learned to walk three times, twice as an adult. I can't remember learning to walk as a baby, but I can tell you that it's pretty daunting as an adult. That may be in part because it seems so much easier to fall! It was hard as an adult the second time around; in fact, I think it was more difficult, because I knew how much hard work it was going to take for me to walk. Self-belief was paramount as the medics had no confidence that I would succeed in becoming mobile again.

How many of you have children or younger brothers and sisters? What strikes me when I watch a baby learning to walk is that they have no sense of failure. If they fall, they may cry for a moment, but they get straight up and off they go again. They simply focus on succeeding, and they keep going until they do. For a start, babies are unsteady and ungainly, but they keep at it until they can walk, run, hop, jump, and do it all effortlessly.

This is an incredibly powerful metaphor for life. If you think about failing or focus on the fear you have of failing, it has a significant impact on your chances of succeeding. You get what you focus on: When choices and decisions are all based on avoiding failure, then the belief that we might fail becomes a self-fulfilling prophecy.

Believe you can and think about what you need to do to achieve it, and success becomes so much more likely. Be prepared to back that up with regular, structured activity, and success will be yours.

Between 1998 and 2004, the progress with my mobility was incredibly slow. I had to look for progress over weeks and months rather than days. I had to keep the faith that if I believed in myself enough AND was prepared to take consistent action, I could learn to walk again. Work was a great distraction from my deteriorating health and a great pain control. Finally, I was given an ultimatum by my consultant neurologist. He told me I had to reduce the large numbers of hours I was working if I wanted to have any shred of quality future. I took the incredibly painful decision to leave the school I loved. They were like a family to me, but I wasn't prepared to settle for a half-life.

In 2004, I had an internal spinal stimulator fitted. Initially, the procedure made me very poorly, but it has been the catalyst for progress with my mobility since then. Progress has been slow. It has required much tenacity and the unwavering belief that I will succeed. As I write this book in the summer of 2017, I no longer need to use the wheelchair in the house or garden. I can now walk short distances, and my pain levels have thankfully reduced. Whilst I still need to use a wheelchair for longer distances, my mobility is the best it has been since July 1996.

It is important to focus on what we can do rather than what we can't.

Let me illustrate what I mean. At times, I have been unable to stand. When I was at home, if the person coming in to help me forgot to leave a cup out, I was unable to make myself a cup of coffee. I could read and watch TV, and that was pretty much it. At work, I could use my brain, my hands, and my mouth, and be a highly effective professional, doing something I thought to be important and fulfilling and that I loved doing.

I had very specific choices to make. I had two options. Option 1: I could have easily focused on all the things I couldn't do. I could have stayed at home and allowed my world to have become very small. Or, Option 2: I could focus on those things I could do. I could get on and do something I loved, be useful, and make a positive difference.

Which would you choose?

We Are All Capable of So Much More

I think everyone is capable of so much more than they think they are. We all overestimate what we can do in a day and underestimate what we can achieve in a month or a year. Those who believe in themselves are not prepared to settle for second best. Their self-belief acts as the fuel to propel their agenda forward. Without self-belief, it is like trying to push a large fully-laden lorry uphill without an engine. You may get started, but it is almost impossible not to roll back to exactly where you started.

The Fire Walk Challenge

Have you heard of or experienced a firewalk? It sounds completely crazy, but the activity requires you to walk barefooted over red-hot coals for about 7-8 meters. However, it can be done entirely safely, without single singe to your tootsies, if and only if, you are in the right mindset.

Despite my limited mobility, I was absolutely determined to do the fire walk when I attended a course run by Tony Robbins, the first of his courses that I attended. On the first day, Tony talked about one of his courses, which was to be held in California. I was really drawn to it, but immediately dismissed the possibility of attending the course, because I believed the logistics of getting there on my own, in a manual wheelchair, were just too difficult. I believed it was beyond my capacity, so I dismissed the idea. The challenge of completing the firewalk was enough.

Everyone filed into the car park. The atmosphere was electric with drums, music, chanting, and a huge pile of coals glowing in the dark. At that time, I could walk very few steps, so I was absolutely thrilled when, with someone steadying me on each side, I managed to walk over the coals with no mishaps. As I sat back in my wheelchair I was ecstatic. I saw the next person to attempt crossing the hot coals was also in a wheelchair, but he was a double amputee. He tipped himself out of his wheelchair onto his hands and proceeded to walk across the burning-hot coals on his hands.

I was humbled. If he could do that, how much was I self-limiting? I decided that I would challenge all my preconceived beliefs about what I could and couldn't manage. Two months later, I travelled to California to attend the course I'd previously dismissed as impossible. My beliefs about myself had been significantly challenged because of that anonymous gentleman. I will be forever grateful to him. Since then, I've travelled to all sorts of places by myself in the wheelchair. Instead of saying, 'I can't do that, it's too difficult', I ask, 'How do I make that possible?'

We all create stories around our beliefs, in which we portray ourselves as either clever or strong or a victim with no control. We become actors in our own soap operas or movie scripts. So, if you are going to write a script, it makes sense to create a great role for yourself. Why not give yourself the role of the heroine or hero, the person who wins, succeeds, and is happy and fulfilled, rather than the fellow who lacks confidence in themselves and plays the victim?

There is a gift in every challenge. The biggest gift to come out of my disability was the emergence of a very different approach to developing leadership, both in myself and in my staff. Necessity is the mother of invention. I had to devise strategies to ensure that everyone took responsibility for their own performance. I couldn't physically get through the door of the majority of the classrooms and those where I could get inside, I couldn't move around easily because of the lack of space to manoeuvre my wheelchair. So, I had to find a way to ensure consistent standards across the school, even though I couldn't observe the quality of teaching first hand. Initially, the training programme I created came about in a piecemeal way, as a result of my responding to the needs as they were identified. Over time, it became structured and sequential. Through it, I taught my staff to take responsibility for their own performance and to help other teachers to grow and develop too.

The training and development programme I designed proved to be incredibly successful. After my school was designated as one of the first Beacon Schools in the UK, I was asked to help many other schools to incorporate the leadership approach I had developed. Its principles and strategies are just as successful in a non-school setting and have formed the bedrock of much of my work since leaving headship, with countless individuals, couples, teams, and entire organisations.

The evidence of the success of my leadership programme with its emphasis on personal responsibility is the fact that my school was twice included in the Her Majesties Inspectors (HMI's) 'Best 100 Schools in England' list during my time as the head teacher. The efficacy of my approach can also be seen and heard in the many testimonials from clients who have found lasting success from using the same techniques. You will find a lot of clients' testimonies about the benefits of my leadership and self-belief approach on the website: www.genuinely-you.com

I know from my own life experience and from working with hundreds of people, we all have the capacity to rewrite our life-story or script. To do so, we need to ensure our beliefs are empowering. If your beliefs are currently not empowering and supporting you in achieving happiness, success, and fulfilment, it is time to create new, more empowering ones.

Competitive athletes MUST believe they have the capacity to win; in fact, they must believe that they are already winners. Throughout their hours of training, they are motivated by the belief that it is possible to win. Muhammad Ali, the boxer, saw and spoke of himself as being the best, long before it became a reality. His unwavering self-belief matched by his consistent programme of training made his claim become reality. Exactly the same principles are true for you, as you face the challenges which face you today.

Now that you have some knowledge about my story, the tapestry of my life, it's time we put the focus back on you. The next chapter offers you an insight into the 7 Underpinning Principles. These will help you to embrace life, and the changes life brings with enthusiasm and an open mind. These principles have underpinned my personal success and the success of the countless individuals, teams, and organisations I have shared them with. Now it's time to let them underpin your success too.

Chapter 2

The 7 Underpinning Principles

The 7 Underpinning Principles outlined in this chapter provide a positive, stable foundation for living a healthy, happy, successful, and fulfilling life. Just like the warp threads in a piece of cloth, these principles provide the structure around which a rich and joyful life is built–moment by moment, act by act.

Learning to appreciate these principles at a conscious level–to be mindful of them–offers you the power of choice. Recognising when things empower and fulfil you, and when they disempower and keep you stuck or playing small, is not always as straightforward as it sounds. Most people are so busy being busy that they take little time to reflect, so they carry on doing as they have always done. It, therefore, becomes their default position.

You need to be actively aware that you have the choice, either to keep doing things in the same way when things are positive and empowering or to choose to do things differently, when they are not. Of course, simply being aware, will change nothing. Real change requires the backing of sustained action if things are going to be different and for the change to last.

Principle 1–Permission

We learn to ask permission as very young children. It is an important element for keeping young people safe and setting boundaries. The practice continues through adolescence and finally as an adult. Seeking permission is necessary and appropriate in the right place and at the right time. Where it becomes a problem, is when we allow what is going on in our heads to act as a barrier to our growth, happiness, and success.

When you think about doing something, whose opinion do you value the most?

Do you think about how others will judge you, or do you do things simply because you know they are right for you?

Giving yourself permission may be a completely new concept for you. Identifying whose permission you consider first, offers a useful insight into the level of freedom and responsibility you give yourself. Permission comes in many forms.

You may have 'that' voice in your head which is, in reality, your mother's, your father's, or that of your boss. It may be the thought of what everyone will think of you that governs your decisions, or it may be your sense of self-worth and what you believe you deserve.

Whose permission do you seek?

Do you allow yourself to thrive and shine, or do you hide behind others' perceived restrictions?

Ask yourself the following questions. Be honest with yourself:

What Permission Do I Give Others?

Do you allow others to treat you in a way that is disempowering or keeps you playing small, a victim, a doormat, a child, someone who cannot think for themselves, or an emotional or physical punchbag?

What Permission Do I Give Myself?

Do you give yourself the permission to treat yourself as well as you do others?

How easy do you find it to say no even when you really want to?

Do you give yourself permission to be vulnerable or ask for help when you need it?

If you answered yes to any of the above, maybe it's time to give yourself permission to rethink and make some changes. Isn't it time to give yourself permission to be creative, loving, courageous, magnificent, playful, powerful, successful, and to treat yourself with respect? To be the best you can be?

Principle 2–Perspective

Perspective is the way in which we see the world–it is our point of view. Our perspective is based on the beliefs we have about ourselves and the world. It is our reality. It doesn't make it true, however much it might feel that way. Learning to challenge our perspective is important, as it provides the gateway into seeing ourselves and the world differently.

Imagine yourself sitting on a train. At the end of the carriage, there is a father with two children. The father seems lost in his own world; he's completely ignoring the children who are running around, making lots of noise and climbing on the seats. You're sitting there getting more and more irritated. From your perspective, the children are being allowed to do what they like, and the father actually isn't doing his fatherly stuff.

Would you feel any differently if you knew they had just been to visit his wife in hospital, and that he had been given the devastating news that his wife was terminally ill and had very few days to live?

Imagine yourself in heavy traffic. Someone is driving aggressively up your boot, tooting loudly, trying to get past you. The likelihood is you would feel irritated. In that situation, most of us would assume the other driver was being impatient and selfish. What we wouldn't know was whether that was really the case. Had they received a phone call to say that a loved one was being rushed to hospital following a serious road accident?

I've chosen extreme examples to illustrate how our perceptions are not necessarily based on the facts. Nevertheless, we make them our truth until something happens to challenge our thinking.

When we are open to it, the introduction of new information can change perceptions, as can the passing of time. However, many people hold onto their perceptions as the only truth, no matter what. This can lead to significant problems at an individual, family, and organisational level, and can result in the huge levels of conflict and violence we see on the international stage.

Learning to challenge your perceptions and recognise the potential of there being a different version of 'the truth,' offers the potential for people to live in a world of tolerance and peace.

As you know, I use a wheelchair, and there have been times when I've been completely wheelchair bound. On my first adventure abroad in the wheelchair and on my own to the course held in California, I was really excited and a bit anxious about how I'd manage on my own.

On the first day, I was told by my team leader to put my wheelchair in a space they had designated for me. As I moved my chair into the space, they put chairs around me, so I was unable to move. That was fine when Tony Robbins was just speaking, but things were very different when he directed the large audience (over 2,000 people) to stand up, and everyone was on the move.

A big part of the experience in Tony's courses is to interact with the other participants. As soon as everyone stood up, I was boxed in. I could see nothing but their backs, and because I was out of their eye-line, people were constantly banging into me, hurting themselves and me. The large screens at the front of the room where films were being shown and information shared were entirely out of view. I felt boxed in, isolated, and unable to take part in any way. I found it very, very, difficult.

At the first natural break, I went to speak to the team leader who had directed me into the space. I was told that I was where I should be. Things were fine as they were.

I tried to make the best of it, but as the day went on, I felt more and more excluded from being a full participant. I got more and more upset.

I'd had such great hopes of attending the course. It had been expensive to pay for the course, the flight, and accommodation, and to hire an electric wheelchair locally. I wanted to participate fully and get the very best out of the experience. It was evident that they were not used to dealing with the needs of people in wheelchairs.

I gave the situation a great deal of thought overnight. I could leave things as they were–that seemed like a non-option; I could go and make a fuss–not my style, or I could attempt to make the team leader change his perspective.

I got up early in the morning and found the team leader before our group assembled. I asked once again to be moved. He was very clear he was not prepared to change anything. I was where I should be.

I asked him, 'Would you give me 10 minutes of your time?' He reluctantly agreed. I asked him to sit in the chair next to me and to stay sitting, no matter what the rest of the audience got up to do. I said to him, 'If at the end of the 10 minutes, you think I'm in the right place, then ok, I won't ask again'.

All the groups took their places. All was fine. Then Tony came on stage, everyone was on their feet, they were dancing to the music, hugging, and waving, the atmosphere was electric. Information was being projected onto the big screens. I had no idea what was written because I couldn't see and neither could he. We were both being jostled by people who were busy doing their thing and quite oblivious to the two of us who were sitting there.

It only took him three minutes to recognise that his initial perception of my experience where everything was fine, was very different to my perception of being stuck. I was very quickly moved to the end of a row where I could use the space to manoeuvre my chair, so I could see the screen as necessary and join in with everyone else, albeit within the chair.

Be prepared to challenge the perceptions you have about yourself, others, and life in general. You may not be basing your perception on all the information possible, but only on the information, you have processed. Be aware it may not be complete or accurate.

Motive

Motives are not always what they seem. It is very easy to assume that we know why people are acting in the way they do. Our judgement is based entirely on our perspective of a situation. I suggest that you question your perspective and the assumptions you make, particularly when they are negative.

It is really common when you have been upset by something someone has said or done or failed to do, to make the assumption they've upset you deliberately. The reality is very often quite different. They've upset you simply because they're embroiled in their own stuff. They are completely oblivious to the potential impact they have on others.

All of us will, at times, act and speak with very little conscious thought. The more challenged we are and the greater the stress we are under, the less conscious we are of the needs of others and the more likely it is that we will miss the clues others are sending out. At some time we have all upset someone else inadvertently through our actions, words, or tone of voice, or because we have done nothing. Consider over the next few days and weeks how often you assume a negative motive from others, rather than working on the principle that people are generally doing the best they can, with the personal resources they have available to them at the time.

Here is an example of where the perception of others' motives can be skewed with a long-lasting and detrimental impact.

I see many clients because they want to develop a more positive sense of self-worth and confidence.

Some of these clients came believing their problems were their parents' fault because their parents constantly nagged and criticised them during their childhood. From their perspective, their parents were critical because

- They didn't like or love them enough or in the right way.
- They could never do anything right.
- Other siblings were the favourite.

These clients assumed there was a negative motive behind their parents' behaviour. They believed themselves to be the victim of unfair treatment by their parents. As a result, they were stuck believing they were not good enough.

In my work as a head teacher, I spoke to and worked with thousands of parents. Based on my experience I believe the vast majority of parents want the best for their children. They want their children to do well in life. Many are keen that their children should be more successful in life than they themselves have been. I think parents are generally doing the best they can. Children don't come with a manual, and sometimes parents get it wrong, at times very wrong, despite their motives being good. I've had many a conversation with parents who believed giving praise would make their child lazy or big-headed. I've known many parents who were struggling to deal with a challenging behaviour, and they lost their temper and told their children how terrible they were. Many parents struggled with their own insecurities and difficult childhoods. Yet, these same parents loved their children and wanted the best for them; they simply didn't know how to bring out the best in their children.

In the situation when a client thinks their problems are due to their parents, I ask the client to think about their perspective of their parents' treatment of them. I ask them to consider the possibility that there may be a different motive to the one they have assumed. Is there a possibility that their parents were acting in this way for a different, more positive reason but were simply unable to do it in a more humane and loving way?

The client's perspective begins to shift. The shift grows as we explore the gifts they have developed as a result of their parents being tough: independence, resilience, tenacity, empathy for others, compassion, etc.

If their parents are still alive, I ask them to consider talking to their parents about their upbringing and the way their parents spoke or acted. We speak about the need to have this conversation in a neutral voice, with no accusation or anger. (That is incredibly important.) Without exception, when clients have done this (and most have), they have been extremely surprised and heartened by the reaction of their parents. Many have discovered for the first time, just how much their parents loved them and how they wanted the very best for them.

Principle 3–Focus

Have you ever noticed that when things are going well, we seem to attract great opportunities, things seem to fall into our lap? The people around us appear to be happy, cooperative, and ready to help. However, when things are going badly, the opposite seems to be the order of the day, it feels as if everything is going wrong, the challenges appear to escalate. Have you ever wondered why?

It has been my observation from my own experience and that of my clients, colleagues, friends, and relations, that whatever we focus on seems to expand in direct proportion to the focus we give it. By 'focus' I mean the time, attention, and headspace we devote to thinking about the situation, person, or issue, and how often we discuss it with others.

We can easily give a situation or problem a disproportionate amount of time and status; we give it our internal focus and back that up with the endless conversations we have with ourselves. The voice in our head goes on and on, and as it does, the issue or problem expands and grows. We compound the situation by sharing it with several others.

Research has shown that we share negative experiences far more readily than positive ones. On average, we tell 37 people when we experience something negative. By contrast, when things go well, we tell on average only five people. Every time we tell someone else, we give energy to the issue. The focus we give any situation feeds it, so it grows more powerful. Our brains are hot-wired in a very specific way. Our senses are constantly filtering the massive amounts of information made available to us through our senses. In any given moment, we have potentially more than 7 million separate pieces of information offered through the senses of sight, hearing, touch, smell, and taste, and for those who are sensitive to reading it, energy and intuition.

When we are functioning effectively, without being overwhelmed, our brains filter the vast majority of pieces of information out. Our brains generally work on habitual patterns. We focus on what we feel is most relevant at that time. Once we become aware of our default pattern of thinking and have an understanding of its implications, we have the choice to keep any thought patterns which are helpful and empowering or to change our focus to something more productive. When we focus on the negative things in our lives, the brain thinks that is what is most important to us. Our filter consistently focuses on negative things, and we appear to experience more and more negative things. It feels as if they just keep piling on. We lose sight of the many positive things around us. This has a detrimental impact on our levels of confidence and resourcefulness. Life feels more and more difficult. It becomes easier to dwell on the problem than on finding the solution.

When we focus on the good things in our lives, on what we can do, rather than what we can't, looking for solutions as opposed to dwelling on the problems, there is a positive shift. Life seems lighter and more productive. It appears that we get luckier, and as a result, better opportunities become available. Of course, there are challenges in everyday life. Shifting your focus doesn't stop difficulties, traumas, and tragedies from happening. What it can do is enable you to feel far better resourced to deal with them.

You are aware how I've dealt with my own significant challenges over the years. Learning to walk twice as an adult and managing long-term health issues and disability has given me plenty of practical first-hand experience of learning how focusing on the positive can make a huge difference.

Focus for Success

If you truly want to succeed, you must focus on your goals. Warren Buffet and Bill Gates, two of the most successful and influential people in the world, believe the most significant reason for their ongoing success is that they focused on achieving their goals and let nothing derail them from their intention to succeed. It is all too easy to get distracted and find 101 reasons not to get on with something. Finding the discipline and focus to see something through, is an enormous factor in achieving success. What you focus on has the capacity to change the quality of your thinking and behaviour, and as a result, the quality of your life. You too can shift the focus and reap the benefits that accrues. Ask for help if you are finding it difficult; it is well worth the investment.

Principle 4–Love

We Have the Choice to Live from a Place of Love–*Positivity*–or a Place of Fear–*Negativity*.

We can choose to live our lives in fear, seeing everything as a threat, fearing failure or success, fearing change, trying nothing new, fearing the unknown, fearing people who appear different, or fearing we are not enough. The list is endless.

There are times when being fearful is both appropriate and life-saving. Fear of being electrocuted stops us from putting our fingers in the plug or touching overhead cables. Fear of drowning because of riptides or strong currents stops us from taking needless risks and keeps us safe. We know how foolish it would be to walk up to a pride of hungry lions. These are the threats which are very easy to identify and where fear triggers a response which ensures our survival.

Perceived fear feels real and immediate, yet it is something we create in our heads. Just like the monsters who lived under the bed or behind the wardrobe in your childhood imagination, fear has the capacity to grow and take over. It keeps people stuck in a restricted world full of anxiety and stress. Whilst the fears are not actually life-threatening in the way lions, riptides, and electric cables may be; they threaten the quality of your life and, if left unchecked, have the capacity to undermine your health and well-being.

Perceived fear and anxiety trigger the same physical responses as actual ones. Even if the fear is only in our head, powerful hormones are released to increase blood pressure, quicken breathing, and ready the body to run away from the perceived threat. The release of adrenaline, cortisol, and hydrocortisone is designed to help us escape. If these hormones are not used up by running away from danger, they persist in the body. Over time these hormones have a negative impact on our health, increasing blood pressure, causing insomnia or digestive problems, and damaging the immune system . . . and so much more.

It would be easy to think that highly successful people feel less fear, yet studies of the habits of highly effective and successful people show that simply isn't the case. They feel as much fear as anyone else, but they don't let the fear stop them. They work through the fear and get on with what needs to be done to achieve the success they desire.

Every one of us will face challenges during our lives, some more than others. It is up to you how you approach each challenge. Will you choose to respond from a place of fear or one of love?

I believe living from a place of love means shifting away from relying totally on your conscious and unconscious thoughts as these are open to all sorts of distortions, conditioning, compulsions, and obsessions. Our thoughts are important, but there is more to living a life of love. Recognise that whatever your background, you are an infinite being, you are connected to every living thing in an amazing world, full of awe and wonder. Living a life through love means owning the amazing, creative, powerful being that is you. Living through love means learning to live from your soul and recognising you have the option to live a life full of possibilities.

Paul Crouse believes that the film character Forest Gump lives from his heart because Forest Gump sees the best in everyone, expects only great things, and as a result, experiences a life which magically flows from one phase to another. He sees life as a box of chocolates. Some are harder than others, but all have a potential sweetness. We have much to learn from him about living in love, expecting the best from others, and giving 100% of ourselves to every situation, however challenging.

Principle 5–Forgiveness

One of the most empowering things that you can do for yourself is to learn to forgive.

Many of the clients I see are holding onto hurts and resentments from their past. It colours the quality of their life moment by moment, but particularly in the area of relationships. Relationships are often damaged because they find it hard to trust. All of us want and need to be loved. We tie ourselves in knots to achieve recognition and gain the love of our parents and partners.

The problem for most of us is that we create a rulebook about how that love should be shown. Unless it manifests itself exactly as it is in our rulebook, we don't believe that it exists. Our parents and our partners don't have the same rulebook as we do; they show love as it is written in their own personal rulebook. There is often a mismatch. As a result, there is a great deal of misunderstanding and hurting going on. Feeling unloved is a common issue, irrelevant of age and gender. People complain their parents didn't love them or that they didn't love them enough or in the right way. They feel let down by partners who don't match their very specific expectations.

Parents often criticise their offspring in the belief that it will make their children try harder or it will help their children make more of a success of their lives than they did themselves. The result is very different as the criticisms erode their child's sense of self-worth.

An elderly lady I know (aged 92) still feels incredibly hard done by her parents. She talks about it frequently; it has coloured the whole of her life and her ability to forge loving relationships with anyone including her own children. She bitterly resented her three brothers going off walking with her father, which they did on a regular basis, leaving her at home to do the housework. At the time, it was common for the girls in the family to be expected to help around the house. Many decades later she is still talking about how badly she was treated; and bitterness and negativity spill into every area of her life.

I have worked with people who have been physically or sexually abused by the very people who are supposed to protect them. When the victim holds onto their hurt and anger, the impact of the original hurt or abuse persists for years after the actual event. Undoubtedly, they have cause to feel that way, but it doesn't serve them well. The act of forgiving frees the victim from constantly reliving the past; it offers the potential of a great present and a happy and positive future.

Holding onto hurt or a grudge is like giving yourself a deadly poison and expecting the person who hurt you to keel over and die. Huge amounts of energy go into keeping the hurt or grudge alive or suppressing it and pretending it is not there. As you can only use energy once, it means that the energy used for holding onto the hurt is unavailable for more positive things.

Forgiveness is not about condoning or forgetting. It is entirely possible to remember, let the hurt go, and forgive the other person. In doing so, you free yourself from the fetters that holding onto the hurt creates.

Many people find it incredibly difficult to forgive; they hold onto the hurt and bitterness, sometimes for years. The problem with holding onto the negative feelings is it does nothing to punish the source of the hurt. Bit by bit holding onto the negative emotions about what once happened creates physical, emotional, and spiritual damage to the innocent party. The past hurt cripples any chance of a happy and successful present or future. It is as if invisible chains hold the person firmly in the past.

Understanding the principles of forgiveness can really help you deal with a situation and move forward. It's important to remember that forgiving is not about forgetting. Nor is it about condoning the act that's led you to feel so bitter and angry now.

If you don't let go of the hurt and bitterness, the original act will continue to colour the quality of your present and future. Letting go is not about letting the other person get away with their actions. It is all about giving yourself the freedom to ensure you get the most out of the present and enjoy your future. It is possible for people to forgive even the most atrocious acts. By doing so, they are finally able to move forward and live happy productive lives.

I've worked with a number of people who have suffered abuse as children. Moving forward from that terrible situation has been incredibly difficult for them, but they have found the courage to do it. They recognised how it would give them the freedom to move forward.

Amy was systematically abused by her stepfather from the age of eight. She was abused by somebody who was in a position of trust. He was a popular man; everybody thought he was lovely. Her mum worked in the evenings.

When Amy cried because her mum was leaving for work, her mum would try to reassure her, saying, 'You'll be fine, Barry will look after you. I'll be back first thing in the morning!'

The abuse went on for years. He systematically abused Amy from the age of eight until she was a teenager and left home. Amy started to comfort eat; she put on lots of weight. (It is not uncommon for people who are abused to turn to food for comfort. Some believe if they get fat enough, they will no longer attract unwelcome advances as they will be too ugly. The belief they are ugly and unattractive persists long after the abuse is over. Others believe if they get big, they will be powerful enough to repel unwanted advances.)

With lots of help, Amy was able to forgive not only the abuser but also her mother for failing to keep her safe. She recognised that to have any chance of a happy future, it was in her best interest to let go of the past and forgive. Amy was able to recognise what had happened was not her mother's fault. She had trusted her husband, and Amy did not disclose the abuse until many years later. By that time Amy's stepfather had died.

Just as importantly, Amy was able to forgive herself for letting it happen. She began to believe the abuse was not of her making; she started to recognise herself as a survivor, someone with huge inner strength.

After years of battling with poor self-worth, lack of confidence, and an unhealthy weight, she's started to recognise her incredible gifts. Her confidence has grown, and she is finally able to get a grip on her unhealthy eating habits. She is much happier, more confident, healthier, and slimmer.

Another client called Jemma appeared normal at birth but started to experience difficulties when she started to crawl. Her muscles were not developing strength as they should. The doctors told her mother to exercise Jemma's weak muscles. Whatever exercises the doctors or physios recommended, Jemma's mother would do far more. When the physios recommended an exercise be done 10 times twice a day, her mother did it 100 times, several times a day in her desperate need for her daughter to be normal. Instead of getting stronger over the years, Jemma's condition got worse and worse. They discovered later that Jemma had a degenerative disease. Her mother's actions actually made the condition worse and hastened the deterioration much more rapidly than it would have naturally progressed.

When I met Jemma, she and her mother hadn't spoken for several years. She was very angry that her disability had been made much worse by her mother. That was compounded by the sense of rejection created when Jemma was sent away as a boarder to a school for children with special needs.

We worked on enabling Jemma to forgive her mother, in order to move forward herself. It was something Jemma initially found incredibly difficult, but the impact of being able to do so has been far-reaching.

In forgiving her mother, Jemma has been able to let go of the corrosive, negative emotions that were tearing her apart. She has developed a much more positive relationship with her mother, and her children now have their grandmother in their lives.

Jemma has been able to recognise that however inappropriate her mother's actions may have been, they were based on her wanting her daughter to be physically better. They arose out of love.

You may think these cases are something out of the ordinary, yet you'll be surprised how many people I've come across who have had something happen in the past that continues to cause them bitterness and hurt in the present. By holding onto that hurt, their lives are more limited and uncomfortable than they need to be.

Even the most dreadful situation can offer us the opportunity to learn something positive about ourselves. You are a survivor. Maybe it is time to recognise and celebrate the fact that you have had the strength to survive. However challenging the situation may have been, there are potential gifts if you are prepared to look for them. The challenge has helped you to become the strong, resilient, amazing person that you are. Holding onto the hurt is like dragging a heavy portmanteau behind you. It's you who carries that load–nobody else. It is your choice whether you keep dragging it or let it go.

Forgiving Yourself

If forgiving others is important–AND IT IS–then forgiving you is hugely significant. Many people hold onto negative feelings about themselves. Doing so does nothing to help them grow or learn the lesson that life is trying to teach them. Forgiving yourself is the greatest gift that you can give to yourself. It gives you the power to move forward, to have a much better quality of life in your present, and a much better quality future.

Forgiving yourself is not about letting yourself off the hook and thinking it doesn't matter. It is important that you take full responsibility for your past actions or lack thereof. The important thing is to put things right if that is at all possible and to look for the underpinning lesson you can take from the experience. Identifying the lesson can help you change the behaviours, which led to the need for forgiveness in the first place.

Feeling guilty has one purpose: to inform us of the need to do something differently. Once the lesson has been identified, it is time to learn it and, if possible, to put things right. Lesson learned; it is time to let go of the guilt and move on. In that context, guilt becomes a very positive teaching tool.

The trouble is that many people hold onto guilt, sometimes for years. They beat themselves up endlessly and play the 'if only' record over and over in their heads. The guilt acts like corrosive acid, damaging self-worth, confidence, and happiness. They stay caught up in an endless loop of guilt and self-condemnation, which does absolutely nothing to put the situation right.

Principle 6–Gratitude

Gratitude is the most amazing, powerful, and positive emotion. It has the capacity to recalibrate the brain by helping it focus on the positive things in life. Recognising the good things in your life, rather than the negative and the niggles, can act as an antidote to sadness, depression, and frustration.

In our busy lives, it is so easy to go through the day without noticing the myriad of wonderful experiences that are open to us on a regular basis. Our focus is often taken up with trying to achieve, worrying about money or what others will think. Time appears to go faster as we go round and round in the hamster wheel we call life. Gratitude is timeless and requires nothing other than our attention.

We have so much to be grateful for. When I became wheelchair-bound for the first time, and things felt pretty bleak, it would have been all too easy to slide into despondency. The antidote was to collect gratitudes. This is a technique I have since used with hundreds of people. Without exception, it makes a profound and positive difference to the quality of your life if you do it as part of your daily routine.

The brain is like an old-fashioned vinyl record. Patterns of thinking are deeply ingrained, just like the grooves on a record. Habitual thinking patterns govern the quality of our thinking and of our lives. This is fine when those thoughts are optimistic and positive, but damaging if they habitually focus on what has gone wrong, what is lacking, or how unhappy we are.

Being grateful on a regular and sustained basis interrupts negativity and begins to establish far more positive ways of thinking. Clients have reported feeling far happier and more resourced within a couple of weeks of starting to collect gratitudes. The change has become sustained over time, allowing them to be far more open to possibilities. Clients report they are enjoying life far more, and problems feel far less daunting than before gratitude became an established part of their daily practice. Some clients have introduced it to their children. It has become a valued part of their bedtime routine.

Don't be fooled by the simplicity of the following exercise. Although it is extremely easy to incorporate into your daily routine, its impact punches far above its weight.

Give it a try! What have you got to lose?

Collecting Gratitudes

Collecting gratitudes is an incredibly powerful activity. I suggest that you incorporate it into your day–every day! It is really easy to do. It takes no extra time, and it will make a huge difference to the way you feel.

During the day look for opportunities to be grateful. Make it easy, look for small things in each day that make you smile, the things which give you pleasure.

The natural world provides an easy way to collect gratitudes. Those I appreciate on a regular basis include the patterns rain makes on the window, cloud watching, a colourful sunset, my lovely garden, the autumn colours, the moon behind the cedar tree at the back of my house, the sound of the sea, or the warmth of the sunshine on my face.

It can be a kindness: someone has let you out into the flow of traffic or opened a door for you; it could be a tasty meal, a positive coincidence, a smile, a hug, or snuggling on the settee with a loved one.

Just be aware as you go about your daily activities. It doesn't take any more time; it is much more about where your attention is focused as you go.

As you lie in bed prior to going to sleep, scan the day recalling the gratitudes you have collected and choose five. By focusing on being grateful before you sleep, you end the day on a really positive note. You go to sleep thinking about how grateful you are.

Actively acknowledge the things or the people who have created what has led to your feeling grateful. Done once, this is a pleasant enough exercise. Done regularly, it builds a different way of looking at the world, one which is more positive and offers you a greater sense of optimism and joy.

Principle 7–Playfulness

Watch young children or animals play, and see them as they learn about themselves and the world. Their confidence develops as they learn, and when they fail, they simply adjust their approach and try again. There is no sense of failing, simply an enormous enthusiasm and sense of joy when they achieve.

It is an approach that works incredibly effectively–you only have to watch babies approach the process of learning to walk, something we've considered once already in this book. No matter how many times they fall down, they simply get up and try again. There is no emotional baggage around not succeeding the first time. They don't care what others think; fear of failure is a non-issue, and they move from their first tentative steps to competent walkers who can run, skip, jump, and climb, in very short order.

As adults, what essence do we lose which makes so many of us feel we 'can't', makes us feel that failing is a big deal, limiting our lives and our aspirations?

I believe that the critical component is playfulness. Through play, our sense of limitation and fear of failure disappear.

Make the decision to engage life with the same optimism and enthusiasm as you did before you forgot how.

Learning to Play

When we play–and I mean play full-out, embracing the joy of being who we are truly meant to be–the constraints which keep us boxed in by our sense of limitation and fear of failure disappear.

If that sounds trite and simplistic, at one level it is. Whilst the principle is a simple one, achieving it can be really tricky, especially when you first start. You are familiar with the saying, 'Practice makes perfect', and that is certainly true here.

You may need some help to identify the beliefs and fears which hold you back from being your truly wonderful, magnificent self, and you may need some strategies to help you to deal with those beliefs and fears effectively.

What It Means to Be Playful

Playfulness is different for each person, but being truly playful should be a positive experience for you and for those you interact with.

It can be as simple as an autumn walk in the woods where you jump in puddles and kick through piles of leaves, or singing along with the radio, playing air guitar, or playing with your children and entering the world of their imagination.

Laughter is an important component of playfulness. When was the last time you chuckled or had a really good belly laugh? Not only is laughter good for the soul, but it also offers significant physiological benefits because laughter eases tension, makes you breathe in deeply, and the body releases feel-good hormones, which combat stress and contribute to creating a positive mood.

Laughter is contagious. It is the antidote to negativity and complaining. Learning not to take yourself so seriously and looking for the humour in even the most taxing situations makes things so much easier to deal with. I have had a huge amount of practice in finding the humour in the challenges created by being in a wheelchair. I know it helps!

The Real Essence of Playfulness Is Approaching Your Daily Life with Openness, Curiosity, and a Can-Do Approach.

Integrating the 7 Underpinning Principles into your life is an important step towards creating a happy, successful, and fulfilling life. They are the foundation on which everything else is built. Each principle will have a positive impact on your life if you choose to embrace it. Collectively they offer you an incredibly powerful combination, which can empower and resource every area of your life, thus making a huge difference to those you care about and work with.

In isolation, incorporating the 7 Underpinning Principles on a daily basis has the power to make a really positive difference to the quality of your life; however, it is when you implement them in combination with the 7 Connecting Themes and the 5 Secret Pathways, that you give yourself an incredibly strong basis from which to succeed.

In the next chapter, we shall explore those 7 Connecting Themes and their potential to help you move forward efficiently and effectively towards the life you want and deserve.

Chapter 3

The 7 Connecting Themes

Connecting Theme 1–Mindfulness

In this chapter, I present to you the 7 Connecting Themes that underpin every aspect of your everyday life. They weave their way through the fabric of your life, facilitating every interaction, decision, and action you take. Interestingly most people never give these things any conscious thought. As a result, the quality of their lives is reliant on habitual ways of being. This is all very well if those habits are positive and support happiness, success, and fulfilment, but all too often our habitual behaviours are less than helpful.

Understanding yourself and how you operate, allows you to recognise those approaches and behaviours which are working well for you and those that hold you back. Many clients have been extremely surprised at how quickly even small changes in the way they implement the 7 Connecting Themes has had a profound positive impact on the quality of their jobs, relationships, and, in fact, the very fabric of their lives.

The first and most far-reaching of the connecting themes is mindfulness as it affects every thought you have, as well as the window through which you access the world. Mindfulness is incredibly important as our thoughts create our emotions, govern our choices, and also determines our actions.

Mindfulness

The quality of our thoughts determines the quality of our life. Very few people actively consider the way in which they think, despite the critical impact it has on everything in life. Our thoughts create our emotions. The way we feel on a moment-to-moment basis is determined by the way we think. Our emotions drive our actions and behaviours. Behaviours based on our unconscious patterns of thinking become habits.

Research has revealed that 95% of our thinking is habitual. Our thoughts don't actually cross our conscious mind, our thoughts stay at an entirely unconscious level. Minute by minute, our emotions and actions are triggered by long-established patterns of thought. Our beliefs govern our thoughts about ourselves and the world, as you will see in chapter 4, which focuses on the Secret Pathway of beliefs, these often go unchallenged.

Our lives are made up of thousands of little acts. Each of those little acts is driven by our thinking. The impact of our thinking is far-reaching; for example, as discovered in a research study, those who think they are lucky are observant in a very different way to those who think they are unlucky. The following experiment has been repeated in highly controlled circumstances several times. The results have been impressive, interesting and completely consistent.

Subjects in the experiment were asked to identify how lucky they thought they were. Each person, in turn, was taken to a house which had a parking bay a little distance from the front door. Before they arrived, different denominations of money had been placed along the path to the front door, some easy to spot, others far less so. The arrangement of coins and notes was identical in every case.

The outcome of the experiment was that the people who thought they were lucky in life consistently found more money on the path than those who considered themselves unlucky.

The research psychologists determined that self-designated unlucky people are closed down to the potential possibilities and are, therefore, less observant, whilst lucky people are more observant and open; they look for opportunities in a very different way from those who have decided they are unlucky. The quality of each participant's thoughts was very different, and so was the outcome.

How you feel when you get up in the morning generally becomes a self-fulfilling prophecy, whether you dread the day or look forward to the opportunities it will bring. We all interpret every situation in the light of our initial thoughts, habitual or mindful. When we are mindful, our points of reference can be changed by new information, and the outcome is often different.

Most of us are unaware of our patterns of language and behaviour and what triggers them. When habitual thinkers interact with and trigger other habitual thinkers, there is the potential for significant difficulty. Patterns of behaviour become established, and as a result, this triggers a habitual reaction from the other person. This unconscious dance can have far-reaching consequences as things can quickly deteriorate.

Have you ever considered how often you do or say the same thing in the same situation without any conscious thought?

How aware are you of your patterns of thinking and behaviour?

How often do they trigger unhelpful responses when you are dealing with other people?

What do you say when people upset you? Do you bite back and say something equally nasty, or do you bite your lip and say nothing?

How often do you criticise yourself?

Do you usually sit and simmer in the corner, and expect other people to mind read that you're upset?

Do you always want the last word? Is it imperative to you that you have to be seen or heard to be right?

It is extremely important for you to recognise that the only person who is responsible for your behaviour and happiness is you. It means taking responsibility for your part in any situation, however unreasonable you think the other people may be. You can't actually be responsible for their behaviour, but you can be absolutely responsible for yours.

Einstein's definition of madness was to keep doing the same thing whilst expecting a different result. We all do it. We do things harder, longer, louder, and more frequently all the time, hoping that this time things will change and be better. Habitual thinking is at the heart of this fruitless behaviour.

Think about a mum telling her children to tidy their bedrooms. Mum says the same thing again and again, but nothing she says works. As she becomes more frustrated by the children's disobedience, she may raise her voice, but the children still do not listen. Not only is Mum in habitual nagging mode, but her children are habitual in their response, which is to ignore her. Her nags have become white noise. Mum doesn't think, 'I've been nagging and nagging and nagging, but it hasn't made any difference so far. Perhaps I'll try something different'. She continues, often for years, nagging, getting frustrated, and feeling unvalued by her children.

It is important that we all learn to be mindful about the way we think. Being aware of our thoughts and whether they serve us, opens up options which would otherwise be closed. It gives us the power to choose! When we are mindful, we can choose to do things in the same way we have always done or to do them differently. Being mindful is the gateway to creating an empowered, fulfilling quality of life and the ability to sustain it, even when things become challenging.

Setting Ourselves Up for Success or Failure

There is a stark difference between people who are highly successful in life and those who are not. Highly successful people have a number of characteristics in common, the most important of which is the way in which they think. This determines whether they will succeed right from the outset.

Thinking about success falls into three distinct categories:

- I will fail.
- I fear I will fail.
- I will succeed.

Every decision will be affected by the person's underlying thinking about success. Actions based upon each of the three categories of thinking will have a very different energy behind them.

If you think you'll fail, it's a done deal. You are scuppered before you start.

People who believe they will fail often don't take any action at all because they believe, 'If I don't try, then I won't be seen to fail'. Their decisions are based on wanting to keep themselves safe. By so doing, they succeed in keeping their options very limited.

If you fear failure, the decisions you make will be fettered by that fear. It is as if one foot is tethered to your comfort zone. The chances of success will be limited by the fear of the unknown. People who fear failure will avoid taking chances, and avoid putting themselves willingly into a situation where there is uncertainty. Their level of success will be limited in direct proportion to their level of fear.

Highly successful people know they're going to succeed. They have an absolute belief that they will succeed. They don't necessarily know how they will achieve success to start with, but they don't need to know how; they just need to know that they are going to do whatever it takes to achieve their goals.

James Dyson, the inventor, offers a great example of someone who was convinced he would succeed. We have evidence that he has done that; he is now a multi-millionaire who has created a wide range of vacuum cleaners, heaters, etc. His success did not come easily. He designed nearly 2,000 prototypes before he had a vacuum cleaner that worked and was ready for sale. Think about all the great inventors in the world and the level of faith they must have had to keep going until they achieved success. When you have that level of faith in your ability to succeed, nothing will get in the way of success.

You may be thinking, 'That's OK, but I don't have that level of certainty'. But, in fact, there was a time when you demonstrated a very similar approach to achieving success. If you learned to feed yourself as a baby, you showed you had an unwavering faith in your ability to succeed. (It may be hiding, but it is still there.)

There's so much we can learn from babies: They have no fear of failure. Initially, they are totally dependent on others feeding them for their survival. Their first tentative attempts to feed themselves result in their dropping food everywhere as they struggle to coordinate their hands and a spoon. Food is spread around as they chase it around their plate, hair, and face. Their bib gets full of food intended for their mouth. Whilst learning to feed themselves, they have no sense of failure; if the chocolate pudding ends up everywhere but in their mouth, they simply try again. Over time they learn how to cut their food up, to handle a huge variety of food, and to feed themselves without any mess. They are no longer reliant on others helping them. Instead, they have become experts in feeding themselves. And this was you . . . This is you!

Think about how often in your life you have made decisions and whether those were based on fear of failure or based on an absolute understanding that you were going to succeed.

Ultimately it's your choice to do things automatically without conscious thought or to think in a mindful way. I urge you to start paying attention to your patterns of thinking; in what situations do you make conscious decisions and when are your reactions driven by habitual patterns? If your way of thinking in any given situation is empowering, then protect it and keep it. If you have ways of thinking and decision-making which do not serve you well, it is entirely your choice whether you carry on in that way or you change to a more empowering approach. Also, you'll find lots of help in this area as you read through the 5 Secret Pathways.

Learn to Fail Better

I find it very interesting how many people fear failure. Why is that so? When I look back on my own life and that of the people I have worked with, it is in our failures we have had the greatest opportunities to learn, develop, and grow.

Think about your own life. Have you learned more when things have gone without a hitch or when things have gone wrong? Enlightened leaders create a culture of development not blame. They expect people to take responsibility for their actions or lack of them. Where learning and development occurs, the process is not deemed a failure. Enlightened people strive for excellence but don't expect perfection.

The only true failures are failing to try in the first place, or failing to learn the lesson the experience offers and repeating the mistake way too many times.

Connecting Theme 2–The Survival Game

Our Unconscious Mind

Our unconscious mind has one primary job–to keep us safe, to ensure we survive. From the moment of our birth, our unconscious mind works to keep us safe. It is constantly on the lookout for any threat. The trouble lies in the unconscious mind's inability to discriminate between real threats to our survival and perceived threats. Fear triggers our survival mechanism, and when it does, our unconscious mind takes over.

Perceived threats are based on our limiting beliefs.

Our beliefs become our reality; they drive the way we think, feel, and behave. Our beliefs about ourselves and the world completely shape our lives; they colour our perceptions; they create our version of the truth. Because our beliefs and perceptions are not necessarily based on actual reality, it is important to assess our beliefs to see whether they are serving us well or holding us back.

Our beliefs fuel our feelings. When we generate fear, it can feel overwhelming and completely illogical.

Fear of flying stops many people from enjoying travel. The fear can be overwhelmingly disproportionate to the statistical threat inherent in flying. For some people, the fear of giving presentations can bring on the same level of stress as facing a life-threatening event, despite there being no reported incidents of death by presentation.

The second challenge about our beliefs is that most of the time, they are running at an unconscious, habitual level. We rarely challenge the validity of our beliefs.

Some of you may be familiar with Susan Jeffers's work. Her book *Feel the Fear and Do It Anyway* has become an international bestseller for a very good reason. The principles of the book are very powerful. Let me share one of the book's guiding principles: If you look at really successful people, the thing that makes the difference in their success is not that they don't feel fear. They feel fear just as much as anyone else, but they don't let that stop them. They get on and do what is necessary to make things happen. You can do the same!

Understanding how fear creates your levels of stress is helpful, as is having a range of strategies to deal effectively with your fears and the stress it has created. It is also important to question the beliefs that underpin the fear in any given situation and recognising the level of genuine threat.

(See the Personal Empowerment Plan at https://genuinely-you.com. It is packed with lots of proven strategies for dealing effectively with stress and anxiety.)

Rejection

Many of our fears are not based on logic but on deeply-held conditioning, which is ancestral. Early humans lived a precarious life. They were surrounded by threats to their survival–wild animals looking for dinner, the elements, starvation, disease, the dangers of childbirth, other rival clans looking for trouble, and so on. The need to be alert and ready for danger was paramount to their survival. Perhaps less obvious was the threat of rejection by their clan.

Being part of the clan was absolutely necessary for survival. It required tribe members to work cooperatively to stave off starvation. Hunting, gathering and growing food, and protecting the tribe from marauding animals and rival clans required collective action. It was pretty well impossible to survive as an individual. Being banished from the tribe meant that you were going to face certain death. In my experience, the fear of rejection is just as powerful in modern-day living as it was for our ancient forefathers.

Common Fears

Knowing your fears and understanding what underpins them is important if you are to deal with them and move forward. Through my work with scores of people, I have found that there are a few common fears.

The most common one is the fear 'I'm not good enough'. It is closely tied to our fear of rejection. It can be dressed up in a variety of ways, but when you get down to the underpinning base of fear, this species of fear is one that runs and often ruins the quality of people 's lives the most.

Other forms of the 'I 'm not good enough' type of fear are

- I'm not pretty enough.
- I'm not sexy enough.
- I'm not desirable.
- I 'm not clever enough.
- I'm not rich enough.
- I'm not educated enough.
- I 'm too short, fat, boring, poor, unintelligent, etc.

The list is endless, but the underpinning belief comes down to the same fear of not being enough. It is actually rubbish. If you believe in yourself, others will see the incredible person you are when you decide to be genuinely you.

Learning that you are good enough, just as you are is incredibly important. You are an amazing, powerful, unique, creative, talented being when you step into being your genuinely best self.

Connecting Theme 3–The Way to Lasting Change

When things are going well, it is important to acknowledge your success and to repeat the pattern of thinking and behaviours that have contributed to your success. When you have identified areas of your life that you don't like, it is up to you to decide to make the necessary changes required to improve those things you don't like or to put up with how things are. It is your choice to change things or to keep them the same. It is entirely in your hands.

Lasting change requires you to rewire your brain. Unless you recalibrate the way you think, it is extremely likely that old habitual patterns will quickly re-emerge, particularly in tough times. Installing new ways securely requires a period of repetition, so the brain can create a new neural pathway. Think of it like this: The first time anyone walks across a lawn there will be little evidence of their passing. However, after repeated passing, the pathway becomes more and more evident. If enough feet pass along the same piece of grass, the pathway becomes deeply ingrained. Your habitual thoughts work in exactly the same way.

You are probably familiar with the saying, 'You can't teach an old dog new tricks'. Until recently scientists believed the brain stopped growing at the age of twenty or so. New technology has given scientists the opportunity to scan the brain in minute detail. We now know the brain continues to have neuroplasticity (the capacity to adapt) throughout life. This is why people with seemingly catastrophic brain injury are able to learn to do a range of activities again. Repetition is the key to success. The result of research studies has shown that people who continually challenge themselves to learn new things are curious, and embrace change have greater neuroplasticity than those who do not.

To create lasting change requires the will to make those changes. It may seem obvious, but many people self-sabotage. At a conscious level, they want to lose weight or stop smoking, but at another, they are reluctant to let go of something the habit offers them. Overeating may provide a feeling of comfort or connection. Smokers who feel reluctant to give up smoking will often see the time spent smoking as 'their' time, an escape from the pressures of the day or as a way to keep their weight down. On some level, they equate quitting the bad habit with totally losing that side benefits which they supposedly derive from smoking, whether it be giving them a sense of comfort, connection, being slimmer or some personal time, even though this isn't necessarily logical.

Marisa Peer, the well-known hypnotherapist, author, and speaker suggests lasting change comes from making the familiar unfamiliar and the unfamiliar familiar.

Connecting Theme 4–The Power of Language

It is extremely common for people to have habitual patterns of language. These can be empowering or quite the opposite. Either way, we begin to believe the underlying message in the language we use.

Here is a very typical example: 'I'm quite good at . . . ', 'I'm quite clever', or 'I'm quite pretty'. It's a way of qualifying things to show you are not being too cocky or arrogant, but by doing so you are not owning how clever, beautiful, or talented you actually are.

In the UK, 'quite' means not bad, OK, almost there. When I recognise that a client has a pattern of using words like 'quite' to dumb down their achievements, I ask the question, 'So if it is quite good, what would you need to do or be differently to make it really good?' More often than not, the client is brought up short. They think for a few moments and then acknowledge that the reality is much better than their language would have you believe. They begin to catch themselves dumbing things down and recalibrate the way they think and talk about themselves.

I'm very aware that there are significant cultural differences in the way language is used. I had a conversation with someone when I was on a course recently about the word 'quite'. In the UK, we use 'quite' to qualify things down. In the US, I was made to understand that the word is used differently; 'quite' means 'very'. The important thing here is to consider whether your use of language is to give yourself credit for your achievements or to dumb down other people's expectations of you.

Think about the language you use about yourself. Do you qualify things, so people don't expect too much of you? How often do you make jokes about yourself? How often do you put yourself down before other people can say something about what you have done? For example, 'I'll give it a go, but I'm not very good'. How many times do you say things like, 'I'm useless', 'I'm not very clever', or 'I'm not very [something]'?

If you are putting yourself down or making light of your achievements, I urge you to start challenging that habit. Over the next few days, you might find it useful to keep a journal to help to identify the things that you notice about your language and when you put yourself down. Awareness is the first stage of any change. You can't do anything about sorting things out unless you're aware that it needs changing in the first place. Please be very mindful of your language and the beliefs that underpin the words you use. Make notes, so you'll be ready to work on those later.

One really good tip: when you know that you have a habitual form of language, it is better to shift it from the present tense and use the past. Instead of saying, 'I'm not good at . . . ', replace it with 'I used to think I wasn't very good at it, but I'm working on it'. By so doing, you take ownership of moving things forward.

The language we use particularly about ourselves has the capacity to empower or diminish us, motivate or demotivate us, help or hinder us. Our brain wants to please; when it hears us say how tired and exhausted we are, it appears to make us feel even more exhausted. If we say how awful a situation is, how it is killing us, the unconscious mind goes into survival mode.

Language has the power to create an intense sense of ownership; it helps to create and sustain our sense of identity. That's great when it encourages us to own our achievements, talents, and positive attributes, but is far less helpful when it focuses on 'my depression, my illness, my panic attacks'. When any problem with your well-being becomes part of your identity, it makes it more difficult to deal with. Creating a sense of distance from the condition is important if you want to move forward. You are not your illness; it is a challenge you are facing; it is not who you are.

One of my clients, Paul, had experienced significant depression for many years. His conversation included many references to 'my depression'. It had become an integral part of how he saw himself. Changing the patterns of his language was a vital strand in his recovery. We downgraded the power of the language he used about his state of mind. Instead of his normal pattern of language, which was 'My depression is killing me,' 'I feel dreadful' or 'It's hopeless!' he was encouraged to substitute these with, 'I'm feeling a bit down,' 'I'm not at my best today,' or 'I'm rather low'.' Each of these phrases was completed with the words, 'But it's getting better [or easier]' or 'I'm working on feeling great!'

Of course, there were lots of other strategies working alongside the changes in his language, but within a month Paul reported feeling much happier and stronger. Another technique he found helpful was the introduction of assertive archetypes. You will find more information on archetypes on the website at: **www.genuinely-you.com.**

Another client, Fiona, suffered from paralysing panic attacks, which governed her life. We introduced a different language strategy for her. We gave the panic attacks a name and a cartoon identity, which was entirely separate from Fiona's. She was asked to draw and name a cartoon character to represent the panic attacks. She created Burt. From then onward, when she began to feel a panic attack coming on, she learned an approach called 'It's just Burt'. As unlikely as it may seem, Fiona started to notice that her attacks came less frequently and lasted for less time. She began to grow confidence in her ability to deal with them. This was only one of several strategies used, but it was an important one.

The language we use particularly about ourselves is incredibly important. Mornings are like resurrection for me. I hurt, I'm very stiff, and I generally feel pretty lousy. I have learned that when you talk about how rotten you feel, you simply feel worse. If you talk about feeling good, it generally makes you feel better. Our unconscious mind follows the language we use.

Dealing with the Harsh Words of Others

How quickly do you react to the criticism of others? Do you bite back, get upset, or withdraw? Are you able to think whether there is any truth in what the other person is saying? If there is some truth in what they say, are you able to acknowledge it and do something about it? What is your immediate view of their motive? Do you assume a positive motive even if the delivery is clumsy? Are they attempting to motivate you or to ensure you don't make the same mistakes they have made in the past? Or do you assume the speaker has set out to hurt or belittle you?

Next time you are on the receiving end of someone's sharp tongue, why not try a different approach? So often we react by saying something unpleasant in reply, and the situation deteriorates. Give the person who is being critical a smile, a thank you, or a hug. You will often get a vastly different response. Sharped-tongued individuals are usually hurting in some way and often respond to life negatively. They often have a poor sense of self-worth and are simply trying to make themselves feel better, or are attempting to feel in control. You can make a real difference to the outcome by the way you react.

Brenda was constantly being criticised by her mother. Nothing was ever good enough, and in the end, my client dreaded going to see her. She found herself feeling tense and anticipating the hurtful remarks long before a planned visit. Mother never disappointed. Nothing was going to change unless one of them began to do something differently, and as her mum was well into her seventies, it was highly unlikely to be her.

As a result of our work, Brenda decided to take control of the situation in a very different way. She realised that her mother's own upbringing and marriage had both been incredibly disappointing to her and that made her very unhappy. Brenda understood that her own reactions were entirely her choice. She could smart and sting when she heard hurtful remarks; she could spend time and energy anticipating the event, being hurt at the time and resentful afterwards; or she could choose to do things differently.

Brenda decided that she would love her mum just as she was. She planned an entirely different approach. She began to see things as a challenge. How many times could she make her mum smile, give her a hug, make her mum feel valued? I am pleased to report that whilst her mother did not change overnight, my client found she felt very differently about her mum, and the relationship improved enormously as a result. The bonus was that her mum did become less critical over time, and their relationship is now far more positive than before.

How often do you say hurtful things? It is important to consider why you do it.

Do you justify it by thinking it is to make the person you are speaking to improve? The chances are it will only make them feel resentful or make them feel even less confident and empowered. If you recognise that you use harsh words, think about why you are doing it. If you really want the best for the other person, there are many far more productive ways than nagging or criticising to motivate and inspire them to try harder to improve.

Whatever the reason, being critical, nagging, and finding fault can become a dangerous habit. It is destructive to the very people we want to help and can sour relationships, all too often with the people we love the most. Being harsh to yourself and others is just as corrosive and damaging to the speaker as it is the listener. This is also true of complaining all the time. The two things often go together. Both habits can be broken easily once you are aware of them. Breaking these habits can create amazing results, improving the relationship you have with both yourself and others.

How quickly do you react to the criticism of others by biting back, getting upset, or withdrawing?

Rather than biting back, think whether there is any truth in what the other person has said. If so, acknowledge it and do something about it. Think about the other person's underlying motive. The motive is often a positive one. They want you to be even better or for you to avoid the mistakes they made in similar circumstances.

Consider whether the other person is trying to feel superior because they have a very poor sense of self-worth and only feel good about themselves when they are putting someone else down. Where this is the case (and it is appropriate), telling them that you care about them or giving them a hug can completely disarm them.

Affirmations

You may be familiar with affirmations. These are positive statements which are said with real conviction on a regular basis several times a day for a period of time. Research has shown that doing affirmations can recalibrate the way the brain interprets the world.

It is important to always express affirmations in the positive. Saying these on a regular basis and doing so with a bit of welly can make a real difference. The greater the conviction and belief that it could be so, the more significant the difference.

The principle behind this strategy is actually quite simple. Our brains are rather like an old-fashioned, vinyl record. You get the same song or piece of music played over and over again when the needle gets stuck in the grooves of an old-fashioned vinyl record. These grooves represent our habitual thoughts, beliefs, and behaviours. When you state your affirmations with real conviction on a regular basis, it acts like someone running a sharp knife across the vinyl record. It interrupts those grooves; the old pattern of thinking gets disrupted, and a new more positive one is installed. If you've had a negative pattern of thinking, affirmations can really help you start thinking more positively about yourself. Remember, you are the creator of your own destiny.

Create a powerful personal sentence to use as an affirmation. It should be stated in the positive and use the word 'I'.

My personal power statement is, 'I am a powerful woman. I choose to be happy and fulfilled'.

I suggest you say your powerful statement as soon as you get up in the morning, and you say it several times during the day. To get an even better result chant it as you're walking. Allow the affirmation to match the rhythm of your walking as it gets embedded into your muscle memory.

Try emphasising each word in turn:

> '**I** am a powerful woman. I choose to be happy and fulfilled'.
>
> 'I **am** a powerful woman. I choose to be happy and fulfilled'.

'I am **a** powerful woman. I choose to be happy and fulfilled'.

'I am a **powerful** woman. I choose to be happy and fulfilled'.

'I am a powerful **woman**. I choose to be happy and fulfilled'.

And so on.

Experiment until you have a sentence which really resonates and feels right to you.

The Importance of Language in Relationships

In any relationship between two people, there actually three relationships going on: the one each individual has with themselves and the one they have with each other. This is true whether the relationship is a romantic one or a relationship with a family member, friends, colleagues, or your boss. Whilst people may be using the same words when they communicate with one another, it is very common for people to have a vastly different understanding of what the words they use represent. This can cause all sorts of challenges.

When you think of the words 'love', 'trust', and 'happiness', what do you actually mean? When partners have a different interpretation of the words they use, it can make a significant difference to the quality of their relationship. When teachers or parents say something needs to be 'better', or bosses say they are 'striving for excellence' or something isn't 'good enough', what specifically do they mean? Having a shared, explicit understanding is vital if communication is ever to be effective.

Connecting Theme 5–Taking Ownership

You Are the Only Person That You Have Total Control Over

By handing over responsibility for your emotional well-being to someone else, you are giving the other person the power and control over your emotional life. Unless you are talking about babies or small children, the reality is that the only person you are entirely responsible for is you. Yet many people hand over the responsibility for their emotions and for the quality of their lives to someone else. In other words, they are choosing to be victims.

If you are in a relationship and you hear yourself saying or thinking, 'S/he made me angry' or 'S/he made me happy', it is important to realise that this is a cop-out. It is no one else's job to make you anything; it is yours. Once you take responsibility for yourself and recognise that it is indeed your choice whether to be angry or upset, to be happy or grateful, the quality of your life will improve significantly. Your emotional state belongs entirely to you. Giving other people the power to decide if you are to be happy, sad, depressed, rejected, angry, or joyful, keeps you in a dependency mode.

Take Full Responsibility for Your Own Happiness

It's far too important to hand over the responsibility for your happiness and wellbeing to somebody else. I think it's vital to recognise that if you're going to give someone the power over your happiness, you have to put up with what they provide for you. And it's a very dangerous route to take. I urge you to take responsibility for what you want and for your own emotional state.

I'll Be Happy When . . .

It is really common for people to create conditions for being happy. 'I'll be happy when . . . ', and they then give a huge list of criteria. For example, 'I'll be happy when I've got that big house and I have my dream job, and I've got a wonderful partnership/marriage and my children always tidy their bedroom and do their homework without being nagged'. The more conditions we need to be met in order to be happy, the more difficult happiness is to achieve.

Once you decide to be happy, it is entirely possible to achieve happiness on a regular basis. It doesn't mean walking about with a grin on your face all the time–unless you choose to. Life can be messy and painful. It is important to acknowledge when you are feeling down, but it is entirely up to you how long you choose to stay there. When you decide to make the best of every day, to recognise and be thankful for the good things in life, happiness becomes much easier to achieve.

Your emotional state is your choice. Take responsibility for that, and step into your power. If you fail to do so, you will be missing a trick. The quality of your life will constantly be dependent upon somebody else.

So how do you move forward? Remember that if you want things to be different, you've got to take action. The quality of your life is up to you. Life is wonderful and precious. My challenge to you is that you choose to take sustained actions to make positive changes in your life. There is much within this book, on the genuinely-you website, and within the Thrive Together Tribe designed to help and support you in achieving the quality of life, you desire. Without your engagement and action, nothing will change. Choose to take control of your life. Identify those things that are working well in your life and protect them. Identify those things that are not working well for you, and make an active choice to do what it takes to change them for the better.

Gina's 7-Day Happiness Challenge

Try my happiness challenge:

- For the next seven days as you get up in the morning, say to yourself with some conviction before you get out of bed, 'It is a new day. It is going to be a great day, and I choose to be happy'. (Doing the 'Funky Chicken' test is optional, but if it makes you smile, it's a pretty good start to the day.)
- As the day unfolds, look for things to make you smile. It can be something simple like watching a child play, a dog running in the park, something from nature, a comment on the radio, your favourite music, or a great cup of coffee.
- Use your senses to appreciate the world you live in. Look at the flowers, the clouds, or rain running down the window.

- Smile at people and watch their reaction. Do it without expecting them to smile back.
- Try random acts of kindness to others without expecting anything in return. They don't need to be anything big. Notice how you feel when you do something for someone else, without expecting anything in return.
- As you go to sleep, look back at the day and choose 5 things to be happy and grateful for. Remember, they don't need to be big things.

Changing Others

Remember the only person you have control over is you. If you want someone else to change, it is important to accept that you cannot make them change unless they choose to. However, if you change the way in which you react and behave towards them, it has the potential to change things. Because your habitual pattern has shifted and you say or do things differently, the other person's habitual pattern will often shift too. When you do the unexpected, it breaks the pattern of automatic response. Let's revisit the vinyl record comparison again (because it's such a good one!): It's like scratching an old vinyl record, which interrupts the regular tune. This, in turn, has the potential to create a different way of thinking and/or behaviour from the other person.

If You Want Change, You Have to Take Action

If you want things to be different, if you want things to be even better, you have got to do something differently. That requires you to take some action.

Over the years, I've been to a wide range of workshops. I've seen people who have spent an enormous amount of money and time going to one workshop after another. Some people use the workshops and courses as the catalyst for change. They get real value from their experience. With others, it is a very different story; despite reading lots of self-help books, watching numerous videos, and attending many courses, it is clear that nothing has changed as a result of their investment of time and money. Their lives have stayed the same because they do nothing differently. They have handed the responsibility for their personal development to the speaker, tutor, or author, and they blame them for their lack of progress. Simply attending even the best course or reading the most amazing book will change absolutely nothing unless you do something different in your everyday life. The choice and the responsibility are yours!

If you always do what you have always done, you will always get what you have always got!

Choose to take control of your life. Identify those things that are working well in your life and protect them. Identify those things that are not working for you and make an active choice to do what it takes to change them for the better.

However good your life is at the moment, things can always be even better. The interesting thing about relationships and life, in general, is that everything starts with you. You are the one constant in every situation in your life. Every minute of every day, whatever is going on, you are the common denominator. You carry yourself into every situation, and even though you may not currently believe it, you are actually responsible for YOU: what you think, how you feel, what you do and say. No one else is responsible for your happiness other than you. By choosing to take responsibility for your happiness you maintain your power.

Remember that if you want things to be different, you've got to take action. The quality of your life is down to you.

Connecting Theme 6–Strength and Vulnerability

Learning to embrace our own vulnerability, to be able to manage the uncertainty and emotional risk that comes with it, requires courage. Many people avoid opening the Pandora's box of vulnerability as the shame attached to not being perfect is simply too painful. Failure to show vulnerability has far-reaching consequences.

Learning to appreciate yourself, striving for growth and development rather than getting stuck in the impotence created by the need to be perfect, is at the heart of being your genuine best self.

Brené Brown, a well-known self-development expert, scholar, and public speaker is best known for her work on vulnerability. In her view, you shut down opportunity when you don't allow yourself to be vulnerable. She describes vulnerability as showing up and being seen, despite the fear of being judged by others as being weak and by your own self as being unworthy.

We look for vulnerability in others, those signs of being human, of having the courage to say, 'I need help' or 'I take full responsibility for making a mistake'. Even super heroes have flaws; these make their characters more attractive because we can connect with their vulnerabilities. Superman with his vulnerability to kryptonite is a much more authentic character because of, not despite, his vulnerability. As a result of the challenges he faces, we connect and care more about him. There is a great paradox–we look for vulnerability in others, but most of us have a very different set of rules for ourselves.

There is a qualitative difference between the need to be perfect and aiming to be the best we can be and striving for excellence. According to Brené Brown, the need to do things perfectly, to be perfect, is based on the need to avoid the pain of judgement, blame, and the shame that being found wanting engenders. It suggests a fear of not being worthy of real connection. She refers to those who believe in their own worthiness as being 'whole-hearted'.

Whole-hearted people live lives full of creativity, joy, laughter, play, and authenticity. Those who are not whole-hearted are judgemental, perfectionistic, always comparing themselves to other people, ranking everything; they play little and work too much; they are constantly afraid and are unable to show their vulnerability. She believes that there comes a time when we become totally tired of proving, pleasing, perfecting, and performing. She says this realisation typically dawns on individuals between the ages of 35 and 55. That has certainly been my own experience and that of the countless clients with whom I've worked.

I agree with her that everyone would benefit from allowing themselves to be vulnerable. It has also been my experience that there are often gender differences at play in expectations. In general, men are frightened of being seen as weak whilst women have expectations of themselves that are completely impossible to live up to. They drive themselves to do everything perfectly and to create the illusion that it has been effortless.

It is important to make a clear distinction between being vulnerable and being a victim. True connection between people is based on trust and respect, which is built up over time. Real trust can only develop if both parties feel safe enough to share their true vulnerability.

Learning to be vulnerable, to let people in, can feel pretty scary. It has been a significant part of my journey–one I am still on. I learned an important lesson in vulnerability when I was doing a course in America. At the time, I was pretty well wheelchair-bound. I always found it difficult to ask for help because deep down I feared rejection. At the heart of this type of fear is the belief that we are not good enough, of being unworthy.

I was taught a very salutary lesson on that day. John, my work buddy on the course, and I were discussing how common it was for people to find it hard to ask for help.

John asked me, 'Do you like helping people?'

I acknowledged, 'I love it. It gives me a real buzz'.

He asked, 'How easy do you find it to ask for help?' I admitted I found it extremely difficult. He got a bit angry with me and demanded, 'What gives you the right to stop other people having that same buzz that you get when you help others?' I thought about it long and hard, and I realized that he was absolutely right. Little did I know I was soon going to have that lesson really forced down my throat in a very strange way.

I decided to stay in California for an extra couple of days after the course to see a bit of the area. I took my hired electric wheelchair to the local mall, as it was just before Christmas, and I wanted to buy some presents. Having finished shopping, I started back to the hotel. What I hadn't bargained for was the steep slope back up to the hotel. It seemed so much steeper going up the slope than I'd remembered on my way down. I was halfway up the drive when my battery suddenly ran out.

So, there I was on a very steep bit of slope, stuck in the middle of the road, with a wheelchair that wouldn't go, and I was totally incapable of walking. The distance was at least a mile long.

I sat in my wheelchair in the middle of the road and waited. There was no one in sight, and I couldn't get a signal on my mobile. Eventually, a yellow cab came up the road and stopped. The driver got out of the cab and approached me. His English wasn't great, and my Spanish is non-existent, but I managed to communicate that I needed help. He parked his taxi and started to push my electric wheelchair up the slope. He was huffing and puffing with the effort.

Within a few minutes, a second taxi drove up. The driver stopped and got out. The two drivers spoke. The driver parked his taxi, he and his passenger got out, and they too began to push my wheelchair, one behind the other, each adding their efforts to get the very heavy electric chair and me up a very steep hill.

Before too long, there were 17 people involved in pushing my wheelchair up the hill–yes, 17! Everybody was laughing. It was a complete spectacle. I learned the lesson that asking for help isn't as bad as I'd thought.

Being vulnerable, asking for help, and letting people know that you are scared may be uncomfortable, but it is not life-threatening. Learning to be uncomfortable in that way will make an enormous difference to the quality of your life. It opens the door to incredible possibilities.

Connecting Theme 7–Faith

The dictionary defines faith as 'having complete trust or confidence in someone or something'. Faith is synonymous with having trust, belief, confidence, credence, reliance, or dependence.

Faith allows a strong belief in the doctrines of a religion or something else based on a spiritual conviction rather than on proof.

Faith means to keep moving ahead even amidst darkness. Faith is walking through a dark tunnel with the hope of finding a candle at the end. It is believing, 'I shall see the next day'. It is the power that makes you believe that someone is there to look over you and make things right for you.

Everyone will have a different view of what faith is and what they have faith in. For some, faith is synonymous with their religion; others have faith in the Universe, Mother Earth, and Father Sky. The object of each individual's faith may vary enormously, but the need to have faith, to believe in something greater than ourselves offers a huge expansion in our thinking and the quality of our lives. Learning to have faith is a real game-changer.

Without faith, life becomes less bearable. Faith is as simple as it is complex. We have faith that however difficult the day may be, the day will end, and the sun will come up on a new day tomorrow. When we have faith that things will come right, we begin to behave in a very different way than if we lack that faith and it leads to incredibly different outcomes. Faith keeps us going when the odds are stacked against us; it offers a sense of hope and possibility, a sense of connection with others.

Faith comes in so many different guises, but it boils down to having a belief that we are part of something bigger and more important than ourselves and that there's a divine power. The tragedy is that rather than bringing everyone together to recognise our connection, people can use their faith to justify the most barbaric and violent acts against their fellow man. I have faith that people have the capacity to come together, no matter what their creed, colour, politics, or religion may be.

Believing in yourself and your ability to cope with life is vital if the challenges of everyday life are not to become overwhelming. Having trust and faith in others makes the difference between a life of companionship, love, and connection and one of total isolation.

I believe it is harder to sustain a sense of joy and fulfilment without a sense of faith and acceptance. There is so much we don't have the science or language to understand; our understanding of things is constantly changing as we learn more, yet the importance of having faith remains unchanged.

Rachel Davis sums up faith really well in chapter 18 of her International Best Selling novel '*The Point Of Me*'. Here, the character, James, is on his second mystical adventure, and he meets his younger sister, Lyra, who appears to him as an aged and timeless woman. James asks her how he will manage to accept his inevitable death. Here's that conversation:

> *'I don't know how to go about accepting, Lyra. I don't know how to give up'. At this admission, Lyra lent into her brother and held her head close. 'Accepting is not about giving in or giving up, James. It is not even about resigning yourself to a pre-written fate. It is about trust and faith. It's about searching for the kernel of peace and love that exists in all things. Some burdens, if not fought against, can make us stronger, kinder. This gives us reason to pause, to think, even to choose. Maybe they even give us permission to make more of ourselves. But it is up to you, James, you have total free-will and it is your choice as to what gives you peace. Do you see?*

We'll return to the theme of faith and explore it in more depth in chapter 8: Secret Pathway 5–Purpose and Fulfilment.

Understanding the significance of the 7 Connecting Themes gives you the opportunity to consider your own patterns of thinking and to recognise which of them are serving your best needs and what needs to change. The introduction of mindful thinking makes an enormous difference to the way you do everything. The other connecting themes have the potential to support effective and lasting changes which will positively support you in achieving lasting happiness, success, and true fulfilment.

With this chapter on the 7 Connecting Themes and the previous one on the 7 Underlying Principles, we have laid the foundation for the introduction of the 5 Secret Pathways. You are now ready to enter the secret pathways to lasting happiness, success, and true fulfilment. You'll find the first of these pathways in the next chapter.

Chapter 4

Secret Pathway 1–Belief

You may have wondered why it has taken so long to get to the 5 Secret Pathways. I could have gone straight to what seems like the main event, but I would have been doing you a great disservice. Sharing the 7 Underpinning Principles and 5 Connecting Themes before embarking on the journey through the pathways ensures you are well placed to get the most out of these pathways. Each pathway is designed to give the perspective, insight, and strategies to empower you in a particular area of your life. You may feel that some pathways are more relevant to you than others, but I urge you to read them all before you decide which of them will have the greatest potential to enhance the quality of your life experience. It is really common for clients to arrive, having identified an area of life they want to change or improve only to discover that there are other issues which need their attention.

The 5 Secret Pathways are designed to encompass all major life experiences. How much or how little you are willing to engage with each pathway is entirely your choice, but remember–if you do nothing, everything will stay exactly as it is now.

Beliefs Create Our Reality

Our beliefs create our reality. Our experiences create the beliefs we hold about ourselves and the world. Beliefs become installed in our brain, and we then give them lasting status. It's great when the beliefs are empowering and positive, but can be disastrous when they are limiting or destructive. We look for evidence to support our beliefs; however, the difficulty is we interpret everything in the light of the beliefs we hold. Our perception of events feeds the beliefs so that they grow in strength as we get older.

Let me illustrate what I mean. Imagine you are in a park; there are two people nearby who have had very different experiences as children. A large dog approaches the first person who was brought up with dogs. As the dog approaches, they welcome it. The dog wags its tail and enjoys being stroked. The person's belief that all dogs are friendly is reconfirmed.

The dog approaches the second person who was bitten by a dog when he was small. As the dog approaches him, he starts to tell it to go away. He flaps his arms and squeals. The dog becomes agitated and growls. The second person's belief that all dogs are a threat is reconfirmed.

It is the same dog, but because different beliefs underpin each person's particular behaviour towards the dog, each person ends up supporting a self-fulfilling prophecy.

One of the most powerful secrets to achieving lasting happiness, success, and fulfilment is the knowledge that transformation takes place when you are prepared to recognise and then challenge your limiting beliefs and the perceptions which underpin them. It is perfectly possible to change any belief that keeps you playing small. No matter what challenges you are faced with in life, it is you that holds the key. They are your beliefs, and you have the ability, power, and choice to identify and then ditch any beliefs that are destructive or limiting.

How Beliefs Are Installed

As tiny children, we are convinced that the world is a place full of wonder and joy. We believe that everyone loves us and is our friend. No toddler has the worry of whether their bottom looks big in their nappy or their hair isn't just right; they are too busy exploring the world. There is no fear of failure. Babies are determined to talk. Their initial babble becomes a game of copycat. They don't care if they lisp, mispronounce, disobey all the rules of grammar, or string together crazy word combinations; they simply want to communicate and get you to understand what they want. Their entire focus is on creating success.

As we grow older, something happens to change all that. Children move from the belief that the world is good, that they are loved and can achieve anything, to a place where limiting beliefs begin to form.

Where do limiting beliefs come from? As small children, we absorb all sorts of conditioning from our parents, carers, and teachers. Attitudes and beliefs towards the way we approach life, the things we value and fear, disgust and shame, our relationship with ourselves and others, money, work, success and failure, risk and responsibility, in fact–everything is modelled to us by those around us. These beliefs are shared through the daily activities we experience and observe, and the language we hear as children. Of course, some of these beliefs change as we grow and mature, but some remain unchallenged throughout our lives. This creates no problem at all when those beliefs are empowering, but it can create havoc to our sense of self-worth and wellbeing when limiting beliefs remain unchallenged.

Survival–Our First Priority

We are hot-wired to stay safe. Our unconscious mind's primary job is to keep us safe. It is the most fundamental of all our needs, and it drives our thinking and behaviours. However, so many of our belief patterns intended to keep us safe have a very different outcome. Because they are often held at a completely unconscious level, those beliefs often go unchallenged. They are manifested in repetitive patterns of behaviour.

Our Beliefs Become Our Reality. What We Can Achieve Is Determined by Our Beliefs

The beliefs we have about ourselves, our self-worth, what we deserve, whether we are lovable and deserve success, are built up during our formative years. I've worked with many clients whose negative beliefs began when parents or teachers told them they were stupid or clumsy. The adult's motive was to help the child to be 'even' better. The message the child took from the remark was 'I'm not good enough'.

When negative remarks are repeated over time, the message becomes stronger and stronger. The belief that what the adult says must be true becomes deeply ingrained. In this way, the child takes that belief into adulthood.

Why is that?

Our lives are made up of millions of small experiences that occur on a minute by minute basis. The brain is constantly on the lookout for evidence to support the beliefs it holds. It interprets each and every situation based on its beliefs. If you hold positive beliefs, the brain looks for the things that confirm how good you are and how well you have done it. If you hold negative beliefs, the brain looks for all those things that support the negative. As you'll find in the example of the financial trader given later in this section, it is all a question of perspective.

If you believe you will fail, it's a done deal. Many people choose not to try something at all because they believe they will fail. In reality, they have failed before they start. Fearing failure brings with it a very different approach from that of those who know they will succeed.

Highly successful people have one thing in common: They have an unshakeable belief in their ability to succeed. They don't necessarily know how, but they will keep working on different strategies until they find one that does succeed. They make decisions based on knowing that failure offers a great opportunity to learn. It only becomes a failure if that learning doesn't take place.

If You Believe You Can't, You Won't. Believe You Can, and You Are Halfway There

I'm sure you have heard of Dr Roger Banister. He is famous for running the first sub-four-minute mile. You may not be aware that before the race, he'd been warned by the medics. They believed that if anyone ran that fast, their body would not be able to take in enough oxygen, and they would die.

I find it incredible that Banister was prepared to take the risk given the warnings. What I find even more interesting is that within a month of

Roger breaking the record, over 30 others had also run a mile in under four minutes.

Why?

Because they believed they could.

Today many athletes have run much faster than Banister. They have all believed it was possible to run that fast and had the self-belief that they could break the previous record.

Solving the Unsolvable

I heard a true story of an American maths student who was unable to make a lecture during his final year at university. His lecturer told him to come and copy down his assignment after the lecture was over, as failure to complete it by the deadline would mean he'd fail the course.

He entered the lecture theatre later that day and looked for the assignment. He saw a mathematical equation written on the board and copied it down carefully.

Over the coming days, he wrestled with the equation, trying to solve it. He burned the midnight oil, struggling to make sense of it. He persevered. He was a good student and believed that if it had been set as part of the course, he should be able to find a solution. Eventually, he found the answer.

When he handed in his assignment, his lecturer could not believe what he saw. The lecturer had put the equation on the board as an example of a conundrum that so far even the best mathematical brains in the land couldn't solve.

How did the young man succeed where so many far more experienced people had failed? The answer lies in his belief that it was possible to solve the problem. His expectation was if he worked at it hard enough, he would succeed. Because he thought it was an integral part of his course, he had no reason to think it was unsolvable.

How often do you sabotage any chance of success because you start with the belief that the task is going to be hard, so 'I won't be able to manage it' or 'I'm not clever [strong, technical, or intelligent] enough?'

The secret to any success is being open to the possibility that you will succeed, that you have the capacity to do it. If you believe it will be easy– that will become your reality. If you believe that's it is going to be incredibly hard even before getting started, then, of course, the brain wants to please you, so incredibly hard becomes your reality.

It may feel like a completely alien concept, but it has been proven to be the case. As we think and talk, we inform the brain of how we want things to be. The brain takes on those thoughts expressed through our language. The brain then works really hard to deliver what you believe. If you'll recall, this also connects to the ideas in Connecting Theme 4–The Power of Language.

Prevalent Limiting Beliefs

Over the years I have noticed there are a number of commonly-held limiting beliefs that affect people from all walks of life.

Think about the limiting beliefs that are currently holding you back. The following list is not exhaustive but offers a few examples of limiting beliefs and how they can impact on your sense of self-worth. Perhaps, you'll find some of your limiting beliefs on this list.

1. Your Self-Worth Is Determined by How You Look.

It is incredibly common for people to dislike the way they look. At one of my recent workshops, I asked the participants to identify how they felt about themselves. I asked them to list the things they liked about themselves. The vast majority of them struggled to get even three. There was a very different response when I asked them to identify what they disliked about their bodies or would like to change about themselves. They scribbled away until I told them to stop. Some had filled their page with a comprehensive catalogue of what they saw as their flaws.

Why do so many people have so many hang-ups about their bodies?

Children run around naked and are oblivious to any judgment about their bodies until adults tell them to cover up. When this is done in a negative way, children learn shame. At times the level of shame installed early in life leads to a completely disproportionate and destructive relationship with their bodies in adulthood.

As they get older, young children start to see and hear negative feedback of how people look from the adults around them. They absorb the sense that bodies which don't conform to society's stereotypes are imperfect. They learn to be critical about the way they look. Small children have no sense that they are being judged by how they look, but by the time they go to school, many of them tend to be judgemental about whether they are physically attractive or not. They learn to be self-critical.

Sadly, many of these judgments are not even based on reality but on images of stick-thin models and celebrities whose pictures have been airbrushed to ensure their version of perfection is achieved. It really saddened me as a head teacher to watch 7 and 8 year olds worry about how they looked. They were already being conditioned to believe that they were not . . . enough. Their expectations of themselves were being shaped so that failure was almost inevitable.

In the Western world, it is common for self-worth to be closely connected to appearance. Of course, there are lots of exceptions. Sadly, the most judgemental people we meet are likely to be ourselves. Self-criticism is incredibly destructive and causes all sorts of problems: depression, eating disorders, self-sabotage, and anxiety, to name but a few.

Judgements about appearance, weight, height, etc., become more definitive and more negative as children get older. The teenage years are filled with the agonies created by not fitting in and belonging to the 'cool' set. The power of the peer group replaces or at least modifies the influence of parents. Having the right look, the right gear, and being seen as part of the group are incredibly important. Children can be incredibly cruel as those who have been bullied at school will attest.

As a teenager, I suffered badly from eczema on my face and hands. I comfort ate and was rather plump. I felt like an outsider, and in a desperate attempt to fit in, I tried too hard. I moved schools several times because of my father's job. I was very unhappy. I felt like a failure and had no confidence. I believed I was worthless. It wasn't until I started teaching and discovered I was very good at it, that things began to change. I made some great friends, many of whom are still close friends today, and developed great confidence professionally.

Many of the clients I've worked with are still carrying the battle scars from being bullied or feeling separate from the in-crowd, even decades after leaving school. The experience deepened their belief that they were not worthy, not good enough. It had become their primary belief, despite lots of evidence to the contrary.

2. Your Self-Worth Is Determined by What You Do.

As soon as I started teaching, I found something I loved doing, and I got great results. For the first time, I had a sense of confidence and self-worth. This was created around my professional life. I knew I was good at what I did.

There wasn't too much time or energy left outside my professional life, so it wasn't until I left headship over thirty years later that I finally began to work consistently on my sense of personal self-worth. When I left headship in 2004, I initially found myself feeling adrift and completely de-skilled. The same feelings I'd experienced as an unhappy teenager returned. Who was I if I wasn't the head of my school? What could I do? What was my role in life? What value did I, Gina, have if I wasn't running my school? It was only then I began to realise that the limiting beliefs about the genuine me, when the layer of professional confidence was stripped back, were not serving my needs. Something needed to change.

I began to recognise it didn't matter how successful you were. If you didn't love yourself and recognise the intrinsic worth of being your genuine best self, then true happiness and fulfilment would be elusive.

Since then I have met many clients who have experienced similar challenges when they have been made redundant, their children have left home, or they have retired. When their perceived purpose in life was removed, there was an immediate downturn in self-worth and confidence. At times the difference can be crippling as professional confidence and self-belief crumble leaving the person feeling vulnerable and worthless. It is the downside of connecting your sense of self-worth to what you do rather than who you are.

We all need a sense of significance to feel valued. Many people achieve that through work. Where there is a high sense of significance and achievement professionally but a poor sense of self-worth personally, it is common for people to struggle with work-life balance. People focus their time and attention where they feel more positive about themselves.

I have worked with many workaholics and their partners. Work provides workaholics with a great raft of positive reinforcement. It can come through a sense of security and control; it offers lots of variety, challenge, a sense of status, and significance, and provides a huge connection to others, as well as opportunities to learn and to contribute. At work, the workaholic feels valued and recognised, and all of these things provide them with a really strong sense of self-worth.

In stark contrast, without exception, the workaholics I know, have lacked self-confidence personally. Those in a relationship were often criticised by their partners for not being emotionally available, for being thoughtless partners and absent parents. Others had a string of broken relationships and some were single and had been for some time. Their response was to retreat to where they felt better about themselves–they retreated into work mode. Of course, it felt like an effective strategy until work stopped.

It is very common for the partners of workaholics to attribute meaning to their partner's apparent lack of interest in being at home. The partner's self-confidence becomes eroded. They believe, 'If my partner loved me if I were good enough, they would want to spend more time with me. It must be something lacking in me!' Solving the problem requires each of the partners to recognise their own limiting beliefs and for them to own their own emotional wellbeing.

It is useful to remember that we are human beings, not human doings. It was one of the most useful lessons of my life, and it is an important element of the Thrive Together Tribe teaching.

3. Your Self-Worth Is Based on What You Do for Others.

How many people do you know who are so busy putting others' needs first that they ignore their own?

Who can you think of, who cares for everyone else but fails to practise self-care?

Do you know anyone who finds it difficult to say no to others because they feel guilty if they do, fearing that the person asking will think less of them?

Many people get their sense of self-worth and significance by doing things for others. Some take it to such lengths that their own needs come way down at the bottom of the pile because they believe they don't deserve anything better.

Most of us like to help others, and of course, it's a great thing to do. However, when you hold the belief that it is only when you are doing something for others that you have value, it can become very destructive.

Imagine yourself as a jug full of water. The water represents your inner resources, including time and energy. When you keep pouring water out of the jug, it will soon be empty, leaving you rushing about, fatigued, and overwhelmed.

Imagine the same jug being filled from a tap. Eventually, the jug will fill and begin to overflow. The jug will continue to overflow if you keep filling it. It is the overflow that should be used for others rather than the contents of the jug. The water inside the jug represents self-care. When you nurture yourself, you will have lots to give others, without becoming exhausted and overwhelmed.

It is fine to say "no," so long as you do it with love and respect. If you are interested in learning some easy strategies to do this with grace, you'll find them in the free podcast section of www.genuinely-you.com

It is my belief that there needs to be a balance. Recognising that each of us has an intrinsic value in ourselves is a great starting point. In my experience, it is really common for people to measure their own value using a completely different set of criteria for themselves to the ones they use for others. Almost without exception, they are much, much harder on themselves, than they are on family, friends, or colleagues. Learning to treat yourself as you do a valued friend makes a qualitative difference to the quality of your life. You will find much more about this in the next chapter, Secret Pathway 2–Love.

4. Your Self-Worth Is Based On Money.

Think back on how your parents talked about money. What were the patterns of language they used on a daily basis about money?

Are any of the following statements familiar to you?

- Money doesn't grow on trees.
- You have to work hard for everything you get.
- Money is the root of all evil.
- There is never enough money to go around.
- The rich are more important.
- I can earn it, but I can't keep it.
- I don't deserve to be financially free.

Each of us creates an internal financial ceiling based on our beliefs and expectations around money, how easy it is to earn money, our attitude towards debt, and whether we can keep money once we have it.

Have you ever wondered why so many big lottery winners find themselves back where they started a couple of years after winning millions?

Why is it that those who are born into wealthy families are often able to build even bigger fortunes than their parents?

How is it that people on similar incomes with similar responsibilities will have vastly different financial profiles?

If you believe that saving and investing in your future is important, you will have a very different outcome from those who believe that you must only live for the moment and who spend everything they earn on enjoying themselves.

Attitudes to debt vary enormously. For some, debt is to be avoided at all cost. They would rather work at several jobs and do without, than get into debt. For others, getting into debt isn't an issue so long as they can have the holiday or the purchase they want. For some, debt creates high levels of anxiety and a sense of failure whilst others feel comfortable with a little debt and see it as a normal part of their lives.

I'm reminded of a client I had some years ago. He was a very successful financial trader. He came to see me because his level of stress and anxiety was causing all sorts of problems. He was worried he might be made redundant. It couldn't get out of his mind that he would be unable to support his wife and two children, he would lose his house, and they would all be made homeless.

I asked him to work with his wife to determine what his family actually cost to run. (It's a very useful exercise to do on an annual basis, whether you face redundancy or not.)

I asked him to create three models:

1. *The Basic Model:* to pay his mortgage, run the family comfortably but no frills; to go down to one car and no holiday.
2. *The Bronze Model:* to identify what it would cost to run the family, keep both cars, and have one family holiday a year.
3. *The Premier Model:* to look at what it actually cost to run the family as it was now.

Several interesting things came out of doing this exercise. The couple discovered lots of subscriptions, membership fees for gyms and clubs etc. which were never or rarely used, and other expenses which actually did nothing to enhance the quality of life for anyone in the family. Out of the discussion came the reassurance that if he did lose his very well-paid job, his wife was happy to get a job to help the family budget.

I asked my client what assets he had to draw upon if the necessity arose. It transpired that he had enough savings to cover level number 2, the 'bronze model', lifestyle for 14 years even if he was out of work for the entire time. My client realised that he would be able to find employment even if it was not nearly as well paid, thus stretching the 14 years well beyond the point when his pension would kick in. As his beliefs were challenged by the evidence in front of him, he was able to let go of all the anxiety and stress associated with his future.

Fortunately, my client didn't lose his job, but he did lose a lot of unhelpful and entirely untrue beliefs about money and what he deserved. He and his wife changed the way they managed their finances too.

You may think to yourself that he was silly to be so worried about his financial future, despite the reality of his situation or that he was lucky to be so well-off. And that's my point: It is our beliefs that create and run our reality. If you believe you are financially at risk, that is how it feels. The brain goes into its primeval survival mode. All the stress hormones designed to help you get out of danger kick in. The trouble is, those hormones are designed to help you run from danger. Because modern stresses pose a very different type of threat compared to marauding animals or rival clans, those hormones stay in your system, making you feel dreadful. Sustained high levels of stress can potentially result in high blood pressure, insomnia, indigestion, stroke, heart attack, or the immune system being compromised. Therefore, it is not just crucial for your emotional wellbeing but also your physical well-being to identify your limiting beliefs and challenge them.

5. Your Brain Cannot Differentiate between Fact and Fiction When It Comes to Your Beliefs.

It is really helpful to understand that the brain cannot distinguish between fact and fiction when it comes to your beliefs. As little children, we believe in Father Christmas and the Tooth Fairy until there is enough evidence to destroy the myth.

When policemen take statements from a group of witnesses, they expect each witness to have different memories of the same event. Some of this will be determined by their physical position as it provides a different view of the event. Statements will also vary according to how each individual interprets information. Some people are more inclined to match up similarities whilst others look for the differences.

Detectives are less worried when there are some variations in the account different witnesses offer than if everyone present gives exactly the same account.

When you are in the process of challenging old, unhelpful limiting beliefs, for instance, a limiting belief around your self-confidence, it can be helpful to know that others cannot tell if you are truly confident or if you are putting on an act. The old saying, 'Fake it till you make it', works incredibly well when you want to change an old limiting belief.

The thinking and the language you use are vitally important. These are two of the connecting themes of the Thrive Together Tribe.

6. Believe It and It Becomes Your Truth: Change Is Possible.

If you believe nothing can change–then nothing does. Nothing will change because you will continue to operate in exactly the same way. If you always do what you have always done, you will always get what you have always got. Change requires two things: the belief that change is possible and action. To achieve something different you have to do something different.

It is really common for new clients to admit to me that they feel stuck. When we explore what has been holding them back, two common factors need to be dealt with to bring about their success:

- Changing their limiting beliefs
- Creating a sustained set of actions

The grand gesture does far less than small actions sustained over time.

7. Life Is Not a Spectator Sport.

To have any chance of winning the game of life, you must actually take part in the game, participate fully, and play the game until the end. You have to be proactive.

Life is not a spectator sport, yet many people sit on the sidelines. Moreover, they often complain bitterly that life fails to give them what they think they want, deserve, or need. Spectating gives many people great pleasure, but it never leads to winning medals.

Like you, I had a choice to make. My choice was I could sit on the sidelines in my wheelchair watching the world go by or get up and live my life as fully as possible, making every day count.

It is all too easy to feel life is so much easier for everyone else or to find your day-to-day routine monotonous and unfulfilling. If this sounds familiar to you, consider whether you limit yourself because you fear getting hurt, being rejected, getting things wrong, or because you fear the unknown or what success might entail.

As a head teacher, I noticed that many children initially chose not to try anything new because they thought it would be too difficult. They believed if they didn't try, they wouldn't fail. Faced with the possibility of failure many children adopted that approach, which then continued into their adult lives.

To get the most out of our lives, we all need the courage to face the risks we encounter. We need to experience new things. Growth comes when we use the opportunity to learn from our mistakes and choose to do things differently the next time. There is no such thing as failure when we choose to learn from the experience.

8. When You Meet an Immovable Problem, What Do You Do?

What do you do when you meet things that cannot be changed, perhaps because of disability, bereavement, or circumstances entirely out of your control? You may not be able to change the circumstances, but by changing the way you react to the situation, you can change its impact. I had to use a wheelchair. I could have seen myself as a victim and felt sorry for myself. I chose to focus on what I could do rather than what I couldn't. To see my wheelchair as an enabler–a chariot of fire rather than a thing of lack.

It is not the challenges in life that define us, but what we choose to do with them. We all face a wide range of challenges in our lifetimes–some more than others. If you can't change the problem, you can change the way you react and deal with it.

As you read the following examples, think about your own experience. How often does a belief about your ability, self-worth, or potential hold you back? Where did the belief originate? Is it empowering or limiting you?

In some examples, the installation of negative beliefs is very easy to identify. However, much of the time the situation is far more subtle. People latch onto a simple remark made with no intention of causing the listener pain. The person is made the butt of a joke, or they make a negative meaning from a situation, but that negative interpretation is completely out of proportion. What I hope you take away from these examples is that it is so important to examine your beliefs and to make a more balanced judgment whether they are helpful or not. Sadly, lots of people never question the validity of their beliefs.

Sadie

Sadie came to me about a year after she had come out of a loveless marriage. They had been together for 25 years and had two grown-up sons. Her husband had constantly belittled Sadie. If she didn't do as he wanted, he withdrew emotionally from her, and it was not uncommon for him to refuse to speak to her for days at a time.

Sadie was staying with her husband for the sake of the children, but as the youngest had now left for university, she felt she could no longer manage the feelings of worthlessness and suffocation that living with her husband had created. The pain of staying had become greater than the fear of the unknown, so Sadie decided to start a new life on her own.

By the time Sadie became a client she had found a house and had moved in. But she believed she was unlovable. She had come to believe much of the negative and unkind things her ex-husband had told her over the years. She believed that she would be on her own forever.

Over the first few weeks of our working together, we examined each limiting belief and worked to shift the balance. Sadie learned to love herself for who she was. She began to recognise herself as intelligent, witty, and kind. She came to realise that she had the most amazing sense of fun that had been entirely squashed in the latter years of her marriage. It was a real privilege to watch her confidence and sense of possibility emerge out of the shadows.

Of course, there have been wobbles along the way, but things have become easier for Sadie as time has gone on, and her sense of self-belief has become positive and secure.

I'm thrilled to say that she started to date and has now found a lovely man who adores her. They are starting to talk about moving in together.

Jade

Jade had just retired when she contacted me. She had enjoyed an illustrious career but had dreaded the moment when she would have to finish work. Jade believed that her worthwhile years were over. She was anxious and confused. What would she do with the rest of her life now that she wasn't working? How would she fill the hours? Who was she when she wasn't being the professional version of herself?

There is often a very strong sense of identity created around the role we play professionally. Jade believed that without the significance and status her job had given her, she had little to offer. It was absolute rubbish, but because Jade believed it, it had become her truth.

Challenging the limiting beliefs which were keeping Jade trapped in a no man's land of unhappiness and limitation was a really important part of her growth and development. Jade believed it was vital for her to find the 'right' thing to do. Part of our work was around her giving herself permission to be curious about what was out there and the will to give lots of things a try before she locked herself into a particular direction. Rather than see any decision about what to do as right or wrong, she began to think there were different choices rather than wrong choices. She began to relax, and instead of worrying about the future, she started to enjoy the adventure.

I saw Jade recently. She was full of beans and told me how much she was enjoying life. She has lots going on and now feels great about herself.

Peter

Peter arrived at his first session with an absolute conviction that he was useless.

It didn't take long to discover that as a child he had constantly been told by his father that he was a waste of space and how he would never amount to anything. Even now when Peter was in his late 50s, his father continued to undermine his confidence, telling Peter that he couldn't make a decent decision and how disappointed he was in his son.

Peter's confidence was very low; he belittled himself all the time saying he was useless. This was despite significant evidence to the contrary. He had a very successful professional life as a highly respected manager. Whilst he was at work, he was decisive and highly organised; he planned strategically, was good at problem-solving, and got on well with his colleagues, his team, and his boss.

As soon as Peter left work, his insecurities came to the fore. They were having a significant impact on his personal relationships. He had a history of broken relationships in which his patterns of destructive behaviour were a significant factor.

Peter needed constant reassurance; he was reluctant to make a decision and left most things to his partner. Partners soon became irritated and left, saying they wanted to be with someone who would be an equal partner. They didn't want to play the role of his mother.

Transforming Peter's beliefs about himself and building his self-confidence have been important steps towards his being able to sustain a loving interdependent relationship. He still has a way to go, but Peter is feeling much more confident about himself. He now recognises that just because his father says these things, doesn't make them true.

He has just started to date again and is approaching things very differently this time.

Keith

Keith came to me because he was tired of feeling anxious and depressed. His moods were affecting his relationship, and he was keen to make some changes. He described himself as being stupid. He lacked self-worth and consistently put himself down.

As we explored his issues, it became evident that he had dyslexia, which had been undiagnosed at school. He'd been classed as 'special needs' and had found the whole school experience incredibly difficult. His best friends had been 'A' students, which made him feel even less successful. He excelled at sport and art and design but felt these didn't count with the school or his parents.

The school curriculum is based on the written word for a huge percentage of the time, making it incredibly difficult for those with difficulty in reading and writing. Where a learning problem remains unresolved, there is a huge challenge for both pupil and teacher.

I asked him to look at what he had achieved in his adult life. He loved solving complex problems in his work situation and as a result was always very busy professionally. He'd achieved professional success very early and had bought his first house at the age of 26. He was now in his forties, a very successful businessman who owned a beautiful house which he had completely renovated to his own design, with 10 acres and no mortgage. He employed several people and was able to go on holiday when he chose. He was happily married and had a son and a daughter who were both doing well.

To anyone on the outside, he enjoyed all the trappings of success. Yet he felt that he was stupid; he suffered from low mood and was taking anti-depressants.

Helping Keith recognise his own self-worth was the key to his feeling good about himself. Learning to acknowledge and celebrate his many gifts was vital. Keith now enjoys a great sense of achievement. He has come to terms with his dyslexia and the challenges it created during his life. He can see that in part the challenges he went through as he grew up made him the strong, resilient businessman he is today. Learning to find alternative ways to achieve things was difficult but has given him a wealth of problem-solving experience to draw upon. He no longer feels low and is off the anti-depressants.

Your Belief Runs Your Life

What you believe runs your life. You believe it first, and then you become it.

Take the time to do a spring clean of your beliefs. Check out whether they are serving you or holding you back. It is your choice whether you stay stuck because of any limiting beliefs. If you want to step into feeling empowered as the glorious, amazing person you actually are, you can challenge and change any belief that is failing to serve your best self.

The Thrive Together Tribe is here to help support you in that journey.

Beliefs impinge on every area of your life, so in our exploration of the second secret pathway of love, I suggest you focus on the beliefs you have about yourself and how they underpin the relationship you have with yourself and others. It is time to let any of these negative beliefs go. The strategies within the secret pathway of love are designed to help you achieve just that.

Chapter 5

Secret Pathway 2–Love

The second Secret Pathway focuses on love and relationships. Life without love is lonely. Research shows that more people than ever before are living on their own, and whilst many live happy and satisfying lives, there is a huge bank of evidence which shows that the level of loneliness is at its highest ever peak. Loneliness is not confined to those who live on their own, as feeling alone and unloved is common even with a partner or as part of a family.

At the heart of feeling loved is having a positive sense of self-worth. Your personal relationship with yourself gets reflected in every relationship you have with others, both personal and professional. It is, therefore, sensible to ensure that you create a positive, loving relationship with yourself.

This pathway is ALL about developing a positive sense of self-worth and a great relationship with yourself. Doing so is just the foundation as it then explores how you can create great relationships with others and finally how to create and maintain a loving, lasting, relationship with a significant other.

These strategies work with existing relationships and offer you a new way to approach new ones. There are lots of examples of how clients have changed their lives and their relationships positively by using the approaches shared here.

Secret Pathway 2–Love

Love is the theme of countless books, poems, and films for very good reason: Each of us desires to be loved and nurtured. However, we all have a particular blueprint for how that should be manifested. When the actions of others don't meet our blueprint, we feel rejected and let down. Whilst many people look for the fairy-tale version of love, the reality is more often than not very different.

The word 'love' is just four letters but has so many connotations: love of self and others, loving what you do, love of God, and living from a place of love rather than fear. When we experience love, it has the power to enrich our lives and help us feel empowered and resourced. When we experience a lack of love, the results can be catastrophic, leading to fear, poor self-esteem, a lack of confidence, depression, and anxiety.

The emotions connected with love and the lack of it are strong and run deep. Those who have experienced a loveless childhood often find it difficult to create loving relationships with anyone including themselves. The problems created when people feel unloved and unlovable will affect the quality of their lives unless they find the strength to take control and change things.

Loving yourself means appreciating who you are, just as you are. It means treating yourself with respect, being able to set clear and reasonable boundaries, being comfortable in your own skin, and learning to like your own company. People who love themselves are compassionate towards their frailties but not overindulgent or arrogant. People who are confident and who love themselves don't need to be pushy or insist they are right. They have an inner strength, a capacity to recognise their weaknesses, and the will to deal with them. Their sense of self-worth is internal and not entirely dependent on others' opinions.

You Are the Common Denominator

As I've already said, you are the common denominator in the whole of your life. You take yourself into every situation you experience. You are there every second of each day from the beginning of your life until the last day; so it makes sense to have the best relationship that you can have with yourself.

Learning to love yourself and appreciate who you are is a really important step in creating positive and empowering relationships with others.

If you have experienced a number of failed relationships, if you find your friendships always fizzle out over time, or life constantly throws up similar troubling situations, then it is time to have an honest look at how you may be contributing to the situation. Taking ownership of the part you play is vital if you are to have any chance of creating a different and more loving present and future.

Every Relationship You Have with Others Is a Reflection of the Relationship You Have with Yourself

Every relationship you have, whether it's with your 'significant other', your parents, children, work colleagues, or neighbours, is a reflection of the relationship you have with yourself. To see an example of this, let's take a look at a particular kind of relationship: that of the bully.

People who are bullies look for those who are vulnerable. I have come to the conclusion after over 30 years of studying children at school and people in the workplace that bullies are unhappy and feel unlovable. In trying to control others and the world around them, they attempt to make themselves feel better; they do this because they lack a positive sense of self-love. Their relationship with themselves means that in order to feel good about themselves, they have to feel powerful and in control. Of course, it is possible to be in a position of power and control without making someone else feel bad, but that isn't the case with bullies. A bully needs a victim.

Bullies instinctively seek out and find people who will allow themselves to be controlled. I'm fascinated to understand what happens in those first few moments when we meet somebody new, and a conversation is started. From the outset, you are giving out contextual clues. You send signals all the time about whether you're somebody who's prepared to be stand up for yourself, ready to set boundaries, ready to walk away, or ready to be bullied. You don't actively say the words, 'I am a doormat' or 'Don't mess with me', but your body language, the tone of your voice, and your responses give a pretty good indication of whether you're somebody who is prepared to be trodden on or whether you are going to demand respect.

I was having a conversation with a new client the other day. She was talking about how her partner treated her and said she didn't like it. I asked her what she did about it. She looked at me for a moment and replied, 'Well, nothing. 'That's how it is'. She had a very poor sense of self-worth. She accepted her partner's treatment of her because at some level she believed she was not worth being treated better; meaning she did not love herself. In her acceptance of 'That's how it is', she was resigned to being treated badly. Someone with a more positive sense of self-worth would not allow anyone to continue to treat them in such a way.

It is important to remember that things can change. Because it's been so in the past, doesn't mean it has to be the same in the future.

Your Relationship with Yourself

The most important and the longest relationship you will ever have is the relationship you have with yourself. This is made up of several elements: what you think and believe, how you receive and interpret information, your emotions, how you behave, and how you respond to other people's behaviours. Each of these elements makes a huge difference to the quality of your life.

Clients come to me for all sorts of reasons, but ultimately, no matter what the issue they present, whether personal and professional, there is one thing that makes the most profound difference to their success or failure. Everything boils down to the relationship they have with themselves. If people believe that they're not good enough, if they don't have confidence in themselves and don't feel worthy, then that generates fear and a sense of failure. If people believe in themselves and have a loving relationship with themselves, the possibilities are endless.

Our Beliefs about How Lovable We Are Have Enormous Power

You read in the previous chapter that many of the beliefs we have about ourselves and the world get installed when we are very young, and those beliefs become our reality.

What we believe about ourselves and the world becomes our truth. People who lived in the Middle Ages believed that the Earth was flat. From this belief, they created a detailed explanation for everything that was going on in their world, like the tides and the winds and the weather. These explanations were based on their truth or beliefs. Because they believed the world was flat, they behaved as if that was the only truth. Most sailors sailed very close to shore because they feared falling off the edge of the world. It wasn't until somebody else had a different belief and was brave enough to test it, that this popular belief changed.

To start with, people were afraid of the new truth. In those days if you talked about the world being spherical, you took the risk of being burnt at stake as a heretic. Only when there was enough evidence to challenge the status quo and a big enough group of people who believed that the world was indeed round, did the beliefs of the general population start to change.

Consider the way babies operate. Initially, they have no doubts that they are the centre of the universe, and they're perfect just as they are. There are no babies who are worried about whether somebody is going to think that they are silly when they pull faces. They just do what they do. Around the age of two or three, things start to change. I'm afraid it is the grownups in the world who start to change things for children. As a result, they lose their sense of innocent perfection, that belief that they're perfect just as they are.

Beliefs become installed by parents, family, and teachers. It's often the odd remark that makes the difference. I'm not blaming adults–they are doing the best they can. Families are very complex. I believe that parents start off wanting to do the best for their children. Of course, the world of each individual parent is coloured by their personal beliefs and experiences.

These, in turn, drive their behaviours and inform the things they think are important.

When a parent tells a child, 'Don't be silly, don't do that', or 'What an idiot you are', the chances are that they are saying it with the motive of wanting to help their child improve. They want their child to try harder. It is also likely that they will repeat the same message frequently.

What often happens is when parents talk about the child being silly rather than the behaviour being silly, the child takes on board that they must be as their parents describe them: silly. The belief that they are silly or an idiot becomes the child's reality. When a pattern of negative reinforcement continues, some children, particularly those who are sensitive, will begin to believe that they are not worthy of love; they begin to believe they are unlovable. Therefore, there will be a direct impact on their sense of self-worth which can carry through to adulthood.

Loving Yourself

There is a significant difference in the responses I get when I ask people to identify what they like about themselves and the things they don't like. Why is this significant?

Most people find it difficult to identify the things they like about themselves. They make light of their achievements, skills, and attributes. They struggle even more when you ask them about what physical aspects of themselves they like and appreciate. This exercise is a very good indicator of the relationship they have with themselves. If they don't like much about themselves, it is unlikely that they have a good sense of self-worth or that they love who they are.

Ask the same people what they don't like about themselves, in no time, they can usually rattle off a long list. Why is that? Why is it that we are so good at finding fault in ourselves and not appreciating the wonderful, creative, and amazing people that we are? When we're our best selves, when we're genuinely who we are, it simply shows the amazing creation in us.

Think about your physical body. What a fabulous machine your body is. You don't have to think about how you breathe and how oxygen is exchanged and goes into the blood. You don't have to think about asking cells to replace your skin or to grow your nails. Most of us rarely think about the incredible range of activity going on in our bodies unless something goes wrong. At our most basic level, we, humans, are incredible miracles.

It is worth taking time to think about the things you like about yourself. Consider the areas you'd like to improve and the things you'd want to develop. Be honest with yourself. If you find it easier to find fault with yourself than you do to appreciate the amazing person you are, it is time to have a rethink and to work on your sense of self-worth. It is time to learn to love who you are.

Making Friends with Your Physical Self

You only have one body during your lifetime, so it is well worth looking after it. It is a paradox that most of us only come to truly appreciate our bodies when something goes wrong. I spent many years hating my thighs, wishing they were thinner, but when I couldn't walk at all, the shape of my legs was of no account. I just wanted them to work properly and without pain.

I'm truly amazed at how many people hate their bodies, particularly women. So many are incredibly critical. They compare themselves to skinny models who starve themselves to ensure they have work. They compare themselves to airbrushed photographs, which have very little to do with reality. It is no wonder that cosmetic surgery is on the rise. Sadly, many people are disappointed after surgery because although the outward appearance may have changed, the inner relationship people have with themselves remains unchanged and negative. This leads to more and more surgical procedures.

Creating a positive and loving relationship with yourself is the first step to creating positive and loving relationships with others.

Clients have found the following exercise helpful in creating a more positive relationship with their bodies.

Every morning whilst you are in the shower, do the following exercise to help you make friends with your body. As you wash each part of your body, go through the following process. It may feel a bit strange at first, but if you keep it up over a month, it will make a positive difference. Start at the top and work your way down systematically.

As you wash your hair say, 'Thank you, hair'. If it's one of the attributes you like, thank your hair for being luxurious, shiny, and glossy. If you don't like that part of you, it is important to appreciate its functionality. 'Thank you for covering my head, protecting me from the elements, and keeping me warm'.

Do you like your legs? Perhaps you think you have chunky thighs or thick ankles? Maybe you think they are too short. Do they work? How would you feel if you found yourself unable to walk? That was my reality, and even now they lack strength and stamina, I'm still really pleased to have them, so I thank them for being there, for joining my feet to my bottom. You may not like your legs, but if you can stand, walk, and run, thank them for their functionality.

Making friends with your body on a regular basis starts the process of feeling better about yourself and coming to love yourself. I've used this exercise with hundreds of clients, and I know it works.

Make the Most of Yourself Physically

Making the best of yourself can help you feel more confident.

Being well-groomed is important if you want to make the best of yourself. Remember, you only get one chance to make a great first impression. Pay attention to your hair, your teeth, and your nails. Take the time to keep them all in good condition; it doesn't have to cost much money.

If you have the means, invest in yourself. Your smile is incredibly important, so think about your teeth. Dentists can work miracles these days with even the most crooked or stained teeth.

Consider the colours that you wear. After I had my colours professionally done, I was absolutely amazed at the how much difference the colour I wore made to how I looked. Knowing I look my best has a direct impact on how I feel so it was well worth doing. The colour analyst I saw determined my best colours by using a series of different colour swatches of material. In yellow, cream, or gold, I looked tired and at least 10 years older than I did in white, silver, grey, and bright jewel colours.

If you can't afford to have this done professionally, experiment in front of a well-lit mirror. Don't wear makeup when you do this as it will give you a false result. If a colour ages you or makes your skin feel dull, don't wear it. I was found to be a 'jewel winter'. Bright, jewel or ice clear colours really suit me. People notice me rather than what I'm wearing. In turn, I feel attractive and well-received. Shopping has become far simpler, and I waste no money on buying clothes, which stay in the wardrobe unworn. It has proven to be a sound investment.

Men, remember wearing the right colours is just as important for you as it is for women.

Look at the styles you wear. Do you wear the clothes or do the clothes wear you? Find your own style, a style which suits you and actually makes you look and feel good. If you are not sure, kindly use a trusted friend to give you their opinion.

If you haven't got a trusted friend with a great fashion sense, use a personal shopper. It doesn't mean that you have to spend lots of money. Most big department stores have personal shoppers available even at sale time. Charity and thrift shops can be a great source of inexpensive clothing too. The important thing is that when you step out, you feel good.

I work on the principle of wearing the right clothes for the right situation. In a corporate business situation, I always wear formal clothes, a suit or smart dress. Finding yourself in a situation where you are inappropriately dressed is a recipe for feeling awful.

A few days ago, I was talking about what I was planning to put in this chapter with my sister. She reminded me of the following incident. As young children, we went to a house that belonged to a friend of my parents. We were expecting to help in the garden and had dressed accordingly. However upon arrival, we found the friend had decided to have a garden party, and everyone else had arrived in their best party clothes. My sister and I were in old clothes ready to dig and grub about in the garden. We both felt very uncomfortable dressed in such old, shabby clothes and shoes. That experience taught me a great deal.

Loving and Cherishing Your Body

Loving yourself means that you want to honour and cherish your body. It must sustain you for the whole of your life, so it makes sense to look after it. Surprisingly, a very significant percentage of the Western world's population fail to take care of their bodies. As a result, many people are suffering from diseases, which could have been avoided. Obesity, diabetes, heart disease, cancer, and many other life-changing conditions would be far less common with a healthier diet and lifestyle. It is somewhat of a paradox that these diseases are on the increase despite the development of medical knowledge and advances in information and education. Why do so many people abuse their bodies? I believe it is no coincidence that the levels of poor self-worth and the pressures to be perfect are both extremely high.

Do you look after your body by nourishing it with the right food and taking regular exercise? Or do you overindulge with food, alcohol, or tobacco? Do you take non-prescription drugs, or take adequate exercise? Do you practise self-care and look for ways to re-charge your batteries and support yourself emotionally and spiritually?

Remember, everything you do is a choice. The impact of your choices affects not only the quality of your life but the lives of those who love you. Obesity is at its highest level ever and is on the increase. Nourishing your body by eating the right things is a great start. Learning to love and accept yourself is the first step towards creating a lasting change where you honour yourself too highly, to inflict damage on your body.

When I started my role as head teacher (principal) in 1984, it was rare to see a significantly overweight child. By the late 1990's we were concerned about the growing number of overweight children, some of them morbidly obese so we initiated a healthy eating and fitness plan for the whole school. It was still a vital part of school life when I left in 2004. Doctors in the UK report finding evidence of weight-related high blood pressure, heart disease, and type 2 diabetes in children as young as ten, and the situation is similar in the US and other developed countries.

Many people live on convenience foods and takeaways, despite there being a proliferation of cookery programmes, kitchen gadgets, and a greater variety of produce than ever before in the shops.

I work with clients who want to lose weight. They have often spent years yo-yo dieting and comfort eating. There is now a well-proven connection between the way we use food and our emotional state. Food is an incredibly important part of our lives. The relationship we have with food is complex as it not only involves the individual but also the family. For many people, the influence is even wider. It includes their community and culture; all have their routines and traditions.

Food is used as a token of love, celebration, and compassion. It can also become a weapon of power and control. Many overweight people use food as compensation when they feel lonely or unhappy, but sadly the momentary pleasure is often quickly replaced with a sense of guilt or disgust.

As already mentioned, people who have been bullied or abused have often used their weight as protection–a survival mechanism: 'If I am big and strong, I won't be hurt, I'll feel powerful' or 'If I'm fat, I won't attract unwelcome advances'.

Do you eat well? Are you overweight? Rather than hating the fact that you're overweight, it is better to choose to make friends with food and have a better relationship with it. Focus on being healthy rather than being slim. That way you commit to long-lasting self-love rather than self-punishment and blame.

Nourishing Your Body Is About So Much More Than Food

If you really care about you, you will look after yourself. Loving yourself means practising self-care: respecting your body, your mental, emotional, and spiritual self, and ensuring you take care of every aspect of yourself. You are worth it!

Think about your relationship with alcohol, drugs, sleep, exercise, and getting out and having fun. Physical activity is vital for health and wellbeing; it is a great antidote to stress. There is a growing body of evidence that supports the need for us to build our mental resilience and that lifelong learning is an important factor in doing so. It also shows the benefits of ongoing social interaction if you want to give yourself the best chance of avoiding depression and dementia as you grow older. Each of these makes a difference to the way you think and feel about yourself.

The old saying 'Laughter is the best medicine' has been found to be true. Laughter triggers the release of the feel-good hormones–endorphins and dopamine–these enhance your sense of wellbeing and have been found to strengthen the immune system.

If you have problems with your weight, you want to drink less, or you're a smoker or you take drugs and want to give up, it is important to get some help. Your body and health are incredibly precious. Research has shown that having a positive and supportive peer group can help enormously, and that's where the Thrive Together Tribe can help by providing support and encouragement.

Looking After Yourself Emotionally

The most important thing is to consider the beliefs that run your life. Those which empower you are keepers, so celebrate them. Challenge any beliefs that limit you or keep you feeling small.

As I've outlined in the chapter on 7 Connecting Themes, the language you use about yourself is really important. Over the next few days listen to yourself and the language you use about yourself, both in your head when you are communicating with yourself and in the way you communicate with others. When you are consistently negative and disparaging about yourself, what does that say about the relationship you have with yourself? Is this the language of love and respect? Does it demonstrate a great sense of self-worth?

Changing the language you use about yourself is the most powerful way of changing the relationship you have with yourself. Your brain listens acutely to what you say, whether it is out loud or the chatter going on internally. It does its best to deliver what it thinks you want.

When someone else criticises you, it is far easier to dismiss than when you criticise yourself. The most important words you will ever hear are the words you use about yourself as they become your truth. Being negative about yourself drains your sense of self-worth and impacts on how good you feel. Of course, there are things you may want to improve, but negative criticism does nothing to achieve that. Constructive criticism where you identify how you can be 'even better' is a far more effective approach. Giving yourself credit and praise is vital for a strong sense of self-worth and confidence.

Remember, you are not broken. You are an amazing, unique person. There is no other being exactly like you. Embrace who you are; love and enjoy being you.

You will find lots more information in Connecting Theme 4–The Power of Language.

Dealing with Negative Emotions

Negative emotions have one purpose–they are a call to action. They are your unconscious mind's way of asking you to deal with a situation which is at odds with your set of values. The situation offers you an opportunity to learn. Once you have learned the lesson, it is time to let the negative emotions go. Doing so is an act of self-love because holding onto negative emotions can be hugely corrosive to both your sense of self-worth and your physical wellbeing.

Many people spend years feeling guilty about some mistake they've made. The guilt does nothing to change the initial situation, and it keeps the person stuck in the past. I'm not suggesting you forget the mistake as there is a much more important gain to be made. However, not forgetting and feeling guilt is very different. Guilt creates a huge amount of pain. In itself, it has no power to do anything other than make you feel bad. It is designed to help you recognise your need to do something differently. It is important to put things right if that is possible and to learn the lesson it offers. Then it is time to forgive yourself and let go of the negative emotion.

Dealing with anger can be a challenge. It also causes huge problems for those on the receiving end. Even if you have good cause to be angry and upset, aggression and violence do nothing to solve a situation. It is like putting petrol onto a fire. No one comes out unscathed, and the damage can be significant and long-lived.

If you are feeling angry, ask yourself, 'What is the root cause?' Anger often arises out of frustration or a sense of injustice. Your anger is providing you with a strong message that something needs to be dealt with differently.

It is always best to get yourself under control before tackling the situation that made you angry in the first place. Remember that when you burn a bridge, it can be a long walk to get to the other side of the ravine. Pushing someone into a corner is likely to make them more resistant and aggressive, and if you fight fire with fire, you simply get a bigger fire. If you remain calm when stating your case, you are more likely to be listened to, and it is harder for the person to wriggle out of their responsibility.

I've read lots of books that tell you to be positive at all times. I think that is not only unrealistic but downright damaging. Burying your negative emotions can significantly affect you, both physically and emotionally. It takes huge amounts of energy to keep negative emotions buried. You then have to deal with the fear of how you will get them back under control if you let them out of the box. It is exhausting! Buried negative emotions have a habit of emerging at the most inconvenient times and in ways which are difficult to manage if you ignore them.

Negative emotions have a purpose. Acknowledging your feelings and being curious about why you are feeling them is a far healthier approach. They are telling you that something needs to be dealt with, a call to do things differently, a lesson to be learned, a fear to be faced. If your emotions feel overwhelming; rather than burying them, get some help and support.

Challenging things happen in life. They can whip up incredibly strong negative feelings. It can be useful to take a step back and give yourself a chance to gain a bit of perspective. Time often gives you a more balanced view of things, as can talking things through with someone you trust.

You can find lots of strategies for dealing with negative emotions and for gaining perspective at https://genuinely-you.com.

Your Self-Care

You have three finite resources at your disposal–energy, time, and money–you can only use them once. Think about the jug in Secret Pathway 1–Beliefs. Do you consistently empty your jug for others, leaving nothing for yourself, or do you keep your jug full and only use the overflow of time, energy, and attention on others?

If you constantly use everything in your jug, leaving yourself constantly running on empty, it is time for a change. Failure to do so will leave you feeling tired, overwhelmed, burned out, and of no use to anyone.

Think of the advice that airlines give you, 'In the case of emergency, put your own oxygen mask on first'. Only when you have a way to breathe effectively, can you be of any real help to the other passengers. My advice is based on the same principle.

One of the most powerful strategies to help you re-calibrate the way you approach life is to treat yourself as a valued friend. This means you must make time to practise self-care.

Being Your Own Best Friend

People often find the thought of being loving towards themselves extremely challenging. One strategy, which has had overwhelming success with clients, is to think about how you treat a really valued best friend and then to treat yourself in the same way. Learning to be your own best friend is a great way to become more loving towards yourself. When you love someone, you want the best for them you care that they look after themselves. Many people take far more care of others than they do themselves. They put themselves at the bottom of their list of priorities. Does that sound familiar?

Most of us have good friends, and we treat them well. We are kind and thoughtful and want the best for them. We are there for them when they need support, ready to listen to their fears and troubles and to be their greatest advocate. When it is required, we can be honest with them, even when it means telling them something they don't actually want to hear. Good friends balance this by knowing when to keep quiet.

As a good friend, we listen when a sympathetic ear is needed and help put things into perspective when our friend has let things get on top of them. We advise them as best we can and do everything we can to help them.

We acknowledge their talents, thank them when they help us and forgive them when they do something we don't like. We support, defend, help, share with them, and think the best of them. We encourage them to be the best they can be, challenge them when they are limiting themselves, and celebrate their successes.

Being your own best friend is all about learning to love and appreciate who you are unconditionally, and learning to give yourself as much care as you would a treasured best friend. I have found time and time again that people have one set of criteria for judging themselves and a completely different set of criteria for everyone else. It is really common for people to be far harder on themselves than they are with others.

Do you treat yourself in this way?

Ask yourself: does a best friend keep nagging on and on and on when you do something wrong? Or when something isn't right, do they tell you that it's not acceptable and why, forgive you, and move on?

I would suggest a really good friend isn't going to be overindulgent. They want what is best for you.

How does the way you treat a best friend compare with the way you treat yourself? Do you give yourself the same care and attention as you do your best friend?

Are you inclined to be harder on yourself than you are on others?

Where do you come on your list of priorities? Do you consistently put yourself at the bottom of the list?

Do you beat yourself up when you make a mistake? Do you learn the lesson and move on, or go on giving yourself a really hard time?

Do you find it easier to forgive other people than to forgive yourself?

Are you more tolerant of others' funny little ways and shortcomings than you are of your own?

Who do you put yourself out for most, yourself or others?

How often do you find yourself saying that you'll help someone else and then find yourself flying around, skipping meals, or burning the midnight oil to give that help? Do you find it hard to refuse others, so they don't think badly of you?

If I asked you to describe your perfect 'best friend' and what made them so, I am sure you would be able to give me a long list of attributes and skills.

Think about weighing up the way you treat and think about yourself and others as the scales of justice.

BEING YOUR OWN BEST FRIEND

Think about the two pans on the scales. Are they evenly balanced? Do you have one set of rules for yourself and a different one for everyone else?

It is important to understand that I'm not asking you to treat yourself better than anybody else but to treat yourself on an equal footing with the way you treat others. Use the same criteria to judge both. Nurture and care for yourself as well as you do your best friend.

Learning to be my own best friend has been one of the most powerful lessons I have learned. I used to put everyone else first. If I made a mistake, I would go over and over the situation in my head. I was really hard on myself in a way I would never treat someone else. I know I am not alone in doing this.

If You Find It Difficult

A number of clients have found the idea of treating themselves as well as they do others very challenging at the start. The more they do it, the easier it becomes until it is second nature.

One client, Angela could not contemplate treating herself as a best friend to start with, because her sense of self-worth was so poor.

I asked about her childhood. Had she had an imaginary friend or a name she always wished that she'd been called? Angela said that she'd always wanted to be called Melanie. I asked her to think about treating herself as she would a good friend called Melanie. Angela found the thought of doing this much easier. Being kind to her alter ego, Melanie, made it easier for Angela to give herself permission to be kind to herself.

The important thing is to treat yourself as you would others. No better but no worse. It is about being fair!

Creating Loving Relationships with Others

Relationships Need Your Attention

Where both parties are 100% committed to making their relationship work, success is assured. Couples who really communicate, who have similar values, and who are ready to laugh rather than blame each other have the recipe for success. They have the resilience to withstand the things life is bound to throw at them.

If you want any relationship to work well over time, you have to give it the time and attention it deserves. When you ignore any relationship or take it for granted, it is easy for things to wither and die. Small gestures–saying thank you or telling people you care about them and value them–make an enormous difference. Your body language and tone of voice are important too.

It is important to consider the part you play in a relationship. Remember, the only person you have total control over is you. It is imperative that you take responsibility for your emotional wellbeing and your actions. You are the catalyst for change if you choose to be.

Shared Values

If a relationship is to work, it has to be built on shared values. This is true for the relationships between partners, between boss and worker, between colleagues, within the family, in friendship groups, and, in fact, within any relationships. There is far more likely to be harmony when people share the same set of values.

Dissent, enmity, fear, and hatred occur when there is a perceived difference in values. Politics, religion, and attitudes towards life, money, or guns can all evoke extremely strong feelings because they represent underlying values.

The fear of difference was vital for cavemen and women; their very survival depended on it. Sadly, our modern world offers countless examples where the fear of difference has resulted in acts of unspeakable violence. I'm reminded of the now-famous words of Jo Cox, the murdered MP, who said in her maiden speech, 'We are far more united and have far more in common with each other than things that divide us'.

Clients who come to me with high levels of stress, depression, and anxiety are often dealing with ongoing situations, where their values are out of step with those of their partner, members of the family, or people at work.

I have found that couples who have difficulties in their relationships have rarely discussed their values. Indeed, many have given no thought to their own set of values until we work together. Not surprisingly, their fundamental values are often mismatched. Love, money, sex, children, family, fidelity, and trust are all examples where a difference of underpinning values can create huge rifts over time.

Just as important as knowing the values of the other person is knowing what behaviours are required to demonstrate that value has been honoured.

Paula and John demonstrated this very clearly.

When we started to talk about their values, at the top of both of their lists was the value of love. I asked them what were the behaviours they needed from the other person in order for them to feel loved.

Paula said, 'I need him to buy me flowers'.

John was really indignant, asking, 'What do you mean? I buy you flowers every Friday'.

Paula replied, 'No. What you do is you put a bunch of flowers into the shopping trolley. That's not buying me flowers; that's just something routine. There's no real thought to it'.

When John thought about what she had said, he could see her point. The flowers in the trolley had been given as much importance as a tin of beans. For it to be a true declaration of love, Paula needed him to go to a florist, take care in choosing flowers he knew she would like, have them wrapped, and then present them to her. It would then be a powerful symbol of John's love, representing the words, 'I love you, I notice you, and I value you'.

When I asked John what he needed in order to feel loved, he said, 'I need Paula to hug me as soon as she opens the front door in the evening. She opens the door and immediately turns her back on me and walks down the hall into the kitchen or the living room. It feels like a rejection'.

Paula was equally nonplussed, mentioning their narrow hall. She explained, 'I do that because then there's no space for you to get past'.

Both of them recognised what each needed from the other, in order to feel loved. Having a shared understanding of how their behaviour was interpreted by the other, opened a dialogue at a much deeper, shared level. Don't underestimate how important it is in any relationship to unpick exactly what people mean. You may be using the same words but mean something completely different.

Intimacy and Affection

Outward signs of affection are incredibly important within a romantic relationship. Don't make the mistake of equating affection with sex. Affection and intimacy are very different, and both are important. Creating a shared repertoire of affection which suits both parties is fundamental to a successful relationship. Successful relationships are built on mutual respect.

Sex can be the most beautiful sharing of love. It can also be used to wound, to wield power and control, to barter, or to block out negative feelings. It can be incredibly special or become meaningless and routine. Where there are significantly different values around sex, it is a source of significant problems.

Many couples experience challenges when they have young children. The demands of dealing with their children, work, the household, and lack of sleep mean their relationship gets neglected. Conversations revolve around the children, and slowly they drift apart. It is not uncommon for both parents to live in the same house but to live separate, parallel lives. By the time the children leave home, they have little but the children in common. It is not surprising that many marriages fall apart when the children leave home.

Creating even a small amount of time to be a couple, to talk, to laugh, and to reconnect makes a tremendous difference. Creating a regular date night when you get together as adults works well. If you can't easily get a babysitter, have a date night at home, cuddle up on the settee and watch a movie, have a picnic in the back garden–any opportunity to rekindle the connection which first sparked your relationship.

Sarah and Pete have two lively little boys, who are a real handful. Both parents work hard, and fitting in everything is a real challenge. I was asked to work with them when Pete reached crisis point and told Sarah he was leaving. She was devastated.

One of the contributory factors to the deterioration of their relationship was that their communication with one another consisted of talking about the children, nagging, and sniping at one another. A big part of the solution has been for them to reconnect and to start communicating effectively. They had both become lost in all the childcare, chores, and professional demands. They have now started to communicate properly, to listen attentively rather than with half their attention on the TV. They have an agreement to turn off all electronic gadgets, so they can spend some time with each other, rather than with a plasma screen, on a daily basis.

Sarah and Pete now have regular date nights. Most of these take place at home after the children have gone to bed to make childcare easier and the costs less. They arrange a monthly night out when either a friend or family member babysits. Despite being done on a shoe-string, date nights have become the focus of much hilarity in both the planning and execution. They have taken it in turns to organise the logistics.

Becoming more openly affectionate on a daily basis has been really important. Making real eye contact, hugging, and touching in an affectionate rather than an intimate way has helped to rebuild connection and trust.

If you feel you have got into a rut, it's time to take action. Be creative, create individual and shared bucket lists. Date nights don't need to cost lots of money. I suggest you create a list of things to do which are a mixture of free, inexpensive, easily affordable, and the occasional expensive treat.

Be creative! Some clients have had great fun planning a date with role play, pretending to meet as strangers, taking a theme and dressing up. If you decide to create your fantasy, it is vital that both partners feel entirely comfortable with what is planned and that there are clear agreements if and when one partner wants to stop.

You Can Learn a Great Deal from Others

Here are some of the common patterns of behaviour I've noticed through my work with clients. The outcomes of these patterns of behaviour cause lots of heartache but can be very easily avoided. As you read the examples, see if you recognise any behaviours you have used with your partner, children, family, friends, or colleagues. Awareness is the first vital step to making changes.

Blaming Others

We're very, very, good at blaming other people. 'He made me unhappy', 'She made me angry'. In fact, you are entirely responsible for your own emotional well-being and for the choices you make. No one can make you happy, sad, angry or jealous unless you choose to let them. Taking responsibility is one of the connecting themes because it underpins every part of your life.

The Need To Be Right Is Highly Overrated

Being 'right' is highly overrated. Just consider that in order for you to be right, you have to make someone else out to be wrong. It is often a very hollow victory as it leaves the other person feeling dissatisfied. And it often leads to problems in the future.

There are times when it is important to get your point across but equally, there are other times when it doesn't actually matter. Choose your battles. Ask yourself, 'What is at stake here? If I let things go, will it be life-threatening? Will anyone get hurt? Does it really matter if I choose not to argue the point?' Where people are dogmatic and determined to have the last word, it says far more about them than it does about you. In my experience, those who hold doggedly onto the need to be right, often have a poor sense of self-worth. Their sense of significance is built on their opinion counting, or on their being seen as the expert, on having the last word. If you are dealing with someone who consistently falls into that pattern, remember that letting them think they are right does nothing to diminish you, unless you choose to let it.

I am right, and you are wrong. A different approach would be to say to your partner, the co-carer to your children, to your mother or father, 'You know what I think. On this occasion, I think we just need to agree that we're not going to agree'. Or 'We have very differing opinions; we're coming from a different place. Let's leave it and find a way to work around it'.

Agreeing to disagree works in certain situations; but in others, it is far better to look for a third way, not yours or theirs, but a different approach that you both create together: a third way where there would be no sense of compromise or loss of face because neither of you feels as if you've given in or failed.

Think about the situations that you find tricky within your most important relationships. How often do you have to have the last word or find you are still fighting as you leave the room? How often do you flounce out and slam the door? Even though you may not be saying words out loud in this situation, you are still trying to have the last word, but in a destructive way.

Expecting Others To Be Mindreaders

People often expect everyone else to be mind readers. This is particularly common when people need help, are feeling unhappy, or need some support.

Let me give you a scenario a client shared with me a couple of days ago. She was really cross with her partner. She had just started a new job, and the partner was doing nothing to help her with the children or around the house.

She explained, 'I returned home feeling absolutely exhausted. I'd had a really exacting day. Everything's new in my job, and I'm finding it very stressful. I arrived home at 6.00pm. My partner had been home since three o'clock, and he was lying on the settee watching TV. Nothing was done towards dinner, and as I walked through the door he asked, 'So what are we having for dinner tonight?' I was really, really cross!'

I asked her how she had responded. She replied, 'I went into the kitchen, and I started banging about. I thought my partner would notice that I was upset and come and help me, but he was completely oblivious. I got even crosser and more upset'. She had expected her partner to read her mind and was even more upset when he failed to do so.

I suggested to her that she might have found a different approach more effective: going to her partner and saying, 'I've had a really busy day. Since I've started the new job, I've been finding it hard. Why don't we both make dinner? Come and help me and we'll get to sit down to eat more quickly'.

I've found that many people fully expect others to understand what's going on in their heads, which is difficult when half the time we don't understand what's going on in our own heads. Please remember, mindreading is something that is better left to the stage performer. If you want somebody to do something, ask them directly.

Be aware of how and when you ask. It is probably sensible not to ask your partner for help in the middle of the cup final if they are a football fan. When you ask, be sure to use an even voice with no edge or whine to it. Don't act the victim; be sure not to nag. Simply state what you **do** want in a very even voice, without any guilt trip. If you are asking children to do something, it is important that your request doesn't become 'white noise', where you constantly nag, but there are no consequences. Children find this very easy to ignore.

'I'd be grateful for your help. Can you do ------- now please?' You'll be amazed at what a difference that makes.

Making Love, Affection, or Attention Conditional

I find it very interesting just how often people use gifts, money, time, attention, or sex as currency to barter for love, affection, or simply giving the other person time and attention:

- *I'll give you my time and attention if you do what I want.*
- *I'll buy you something nice if you do what I want.*
- *You can have sex with me if you do what I want.*

Most of the time bartering is done more subtly, but when you look at the underpinning behaviours, they boil down to 'I'll give you what you need if you do what I want'.

It is an approach often learned at childhood. Children see their parents modelling these behaviours with one another, and their parents use bribery as a way to get what they want from them and their siblings.

Conditional love can be very destructive over time. It erodes self-worth and confidence. Those on the receiving end start to believe they only have worth when they are pleasing others. It creates a dependency model of love.

Of course, there are times when bribing your children can be a helpful short-term strategy. There is a subtle but important difference between rewarding children to help them be motivated to do their homework for example, which is in their best interest and using bribery to gain time or love and attention. It is then likely to create a sense of being unworthy in the long term.

A far better approach is to teach your child the principle of cause and consequence, quite separately to your demonstrating that you love them. Love should be given unconditionally. 'I love you very much, but I don't like the way you are behaving. I don't expect you to behave in that way. You are too clever/sensible/lovely/helpful' is a way of speaking that separates the behaviour from love.

If you make your love conditional, it's going to be a very different and much less satisfying form of love than unconditional love.

Wanting to Change Your Partner

One of the common patterns I see in people who have experienced several failed relationships is for one partner to believe they can change the other. In the first flush of the new relationship, everything feels rosy. They're really happy about the new relationship; they enjoy being with that person. However, within a few days, weeks, or months they're trying to change that person to something they're not. At times the change they want would require a complete metamorphosis into a different personality.

Sharon came to me because she'd had a series of failed relationships, which were very destructive. They left her feeling worthless and alone. When we started to look at the underlying patterns of her relationships, it was clear there were some common issues. Sharon had been looking for a man who would take care of her. She wanted a man who was strong, one who was going to take charge, initiate, and organise holidays and social activities, and take care of the upkeep and repairs around the house.

The reality was when partners were strong and decisive, Sharon found them controlling. When they arranged things, she often found fault. If they were not strong and decisive and didn't measure up to Sharon's blueprint, she found them weak. Over-controlling or weak but never just right, a bit like Goldilocks and the three bears. Sharon then spent the next few weeks and months trying and failing to change her partner, and eventually, each relationship came to a challenging end.

Recognising the pattern was the first step for Sharon. She identified the values which were important to her and why. She considered what was important to her in relation to a partner, and it became very clear what was negotiable and what was not. She took responsibility for herself and her behaviour. What sort of partner did she need to be, to match the sort of partner she wanted? It was important for her to create a more positive relationship with herself and for her to recognise how her patterns of behaviour could enhance or destroy any future relationship.

Armed with these insights, Sharon began to use a different approach. She learned to recognise the importance of managing her own emotional state and not relying on someone else to make her happy.

As a result, Sharon is now dating again, and the early signs are extremely promising. She is far more confident and far less demanding.

Being a Victim

Louise came to me after a string of terrible relationships left her feeling emotionally bruised and with little confidence. Through our discussion, it became clear she always went for the good-looking bad boys. Louise liked those who looked slick and sounded clever, who drove fast cars. Dating them initially felt thrilling until they began to treat her badly. Once in the relationship, she would immediately become somebody who was simpering and clingy: she became a victim. She created no boundaries, giving partners tacit permission to treat her badly.

When we started working together, one of the things I asked her to think about was the pattern of choices she had made in the past. I asked her to consider the type of men she had chosen and to look at how she behaved with her partner when she went into a relationship. Developing an awareness of those patterns of behaviour would give Louise the opportunity to consider which behaviours and tendencies to maintain and which to change.

Having a set of simple strategies to help her make those changes was imperative if she was to create a long-term relationship based on love and respect. We worked on how she could change not only her choices but her patterns of behaviour once she had made her initial choice. Ongoing support helped whilst she initiated and embedded those changes, making success far more achievable.

The upshot is she has now met a guy who is very different to all her previous boyfriends. Her present partner isn't flashy. He is someone who is kind and considerate. It has taken quite an adjustment for Louise to believe she deserves to be treated well, but she has made huge strides. Louise and her partner are now living together and are both very happy. Their relationship is built on interdependence and not dependence. They treat each other lovingly and respectfully. Louise is confident and expects to be treated well. She is a long way from the clingy victim of previous relationships.

You are the arbiter of the quality of your life. If you don't like how your life is going, you have the choice to take action and change it or to stay stuck where you are.

Living a Life of Love Rather Than Fear

Fear and love are polar opposites. Learning to live a heart-centred life, governed by love rather than fear, is an important facet of living a life of purpose and fulfilment, a theme we'll explore later, in chapter 8 Secret Pathway 5– Purpose and Fulfilment.

To feel happy, successful, and truly fulfilled it is vital to love and accept yourself. Without a strong sense of self-worth, it will always feel as if something is missing from your life. That sense of lack leads to unhappiness and dissatisfaction, which no amount of external intervention will satisfy. It is, in my opinion, why so many people use food, alcohol, drugs, shopping, sex, or some other external antidote in a bid to satisfy themselves. The momentary satisfaction is quickly replaced by the underlying unhappiness, and so the cycle continues.

Having a great sense of self-worth is important if you want to achieve lasting success. It makes a huge difference in EVERY relationship you have in life both personal and professional. Because of that, it is important that you learn to love and accept yourself in order to achieve the success you dream of. It is entirely possible for you to achieve significant and lasting success, which I'll reveal in the next chapter, Secret Pathway 3–Success.

Chapter 6

Secret Pathway 3–Success

What do we mean by success? Everyone will have a different definition of what success means for them. Of course, there are common themes, but it is important that you decide on your own definition. Just as important is having a clear sense of what that success will look and feel like once you have achieved it. Unless you do that, it is really difficult to plan, to recognise progress, and to know when you have arrived.

Secret Pathway 3 is based on a great deal of research around what the differences are between those who are highly successful on a consistent basis and those who dream of success but find it hard to achieve it at all or who gain fleeting success but are unable to sustain it. I share my own approach, which has worked for me and for my clients. I know it works, but you have to be prepared to take sustained action. Even small changes can make a huge difference if you do them consistently.

To achieve a state of happiness, success, and true fulfilment, it is important for you to be the arbiter of how you define success. It is one of the reasons why Secret Pathway 2 focused on loving and appreciating who you are. Without that, no amount of financial, professional, or personal success will ever be enough to fill the void that poor self-worth or a lack of self-worth creates.

The Enlightened Optimist

There has been a lot of research carried out at Harvard over the last 25 years, which shows that happy, optimistic people are the most successful in life. It is a concept, which is anything but fluffy. To be an enlightened optimist requires self-awareness, self-discipline, toughness, resilience, and focus. Enlightened optimists are also able to share their sense of hope and possibility with others. This is particularly important in times of challenge and change.

Research has shown that pessimists focus on the problem. They are consistently in survival mode. When things go wrong, they lament, 'Why me?' They look for causes to blame, and there is a sense of the difficulty being permanent. When things do go well, there is a belief that it is just temporary, and trouble is just around the corner.

Optimists focus on the solution. They are constantly in progress mode. They look for and embrace change, wondering, 'So, what's next?' They see setbacks as temporary and good things as permanent. Optimists smile more; they create and maintain rapport more easily. Their approach is built on 'I can', and they are ready to offer and consider options.

Do you look to yourself or blame others when things don't go to plan?

Do you see problems as insurmountable or a bit of a setback?

Do you think, 'It's all ruined!'? Or do you identify the specific thing, which has gone wrong, and take steps to put it right?

I have been asked whether a person is born an optimist or a pessimist and whether it is possible to change your approach to life. I know that some people appear to be more predisposed to an optimistic approach to life; however, it is possible to develop greater optimism if you are mindful about the way you think.

Everything you do is a choice. When things are out of your control, you have the choice as to how you react to things.

The first step is to become self-aware:

Be aware of the way you think. Be aware of the impact you have on others. Be aware of your body language, the tone of your voice, and the words you use. Be really honest about your motives and how you interpret what others do and say. Watch how your words land on others.

Your Beliefs Underpin Your Success

Let's revisit a key message of this book: You are the common denominator of every situation in your life. You take yourself into every situation. All of us create stories about ourselves based on our beliefs. We talked in detail about beliefs in Secret Pathway 1 since having empowering beliefs is crucial if you want to succeed consistently. When you believe in yourself, you create a story where you are empowered. However, if you don't believe in yourself, it's very easy to get stuck in a pattern of being a victim. If you're going to create the script for the story of your life, why not write yourself a fabulous part and give yourself the role of the hero or heroine?

Highly successful people have one thing in common: They believe they will succeed. They don't always know how, but they have an unwavering faith that they will find the way to succeed no matter how many setbacks they experience. Failure is simply another opportunity to learn, another step towards achieving their goal. They are clear about what they want to achieve and why it is important to them. They take action towards their goal on a daily basis and let nothing deflect them from their ultimate goal.

There are countless examples of highly successful people who have a whole series of failed attempts before they achieve the success they desire. I wonder how many people have given up when their desired goal was in sight. We'll never know. What we do know is that unsuccessful people will give up when it gets uncomfortable; they would rather stay in their comfort zone and deal with what is familiar.

Fearing Failure–Fearing Success

Edison said, 'I have not failed. I've just found 10,000 ways which won't work'.

Many people fear failure, but in my experience, I have found that almost as many fear success. They have a belief that if they succeed and do well, they'll be seen to be arrogant and boastful or that people won't like them anymore. They may fear that their family or peer group will reject them if they start to behave differently. They may believe that they are not worthy of success and all its trappings. Whatever the limiting belief may be, unless it is dealt with, the belief is likely to sabotage any attempts to succeed consistently.

You may be familiar with this famous poem by Marianne Williamson.

Our Deepest Fear

Our deepest fear is not that we're inadequate.

Our deepest fear is that we're powerful beyond measure.

It's our light, not our darkness that most frightens us.

We ask ourselves, Who am I to be brilliant, gorgeous, talented, fabulous?

Actually, who are you not to be?

You are a child of God.

Your playing small does not serve the world.

There is nothing enlightened about shrinking so that other people won't feel insecure around you.

We are all meant to shine, as children do.

We were born to make manifest the glory of God that is within us.

It's not just in some others; it's in everyone.

And as we let our own light shine, we unconsciously give other people permission to do the same.

As we're liberated from our own fear, our presence automatically liberates others.

I'm asking you to give yourself permission to shine, not only for yourself, although that is incredibly important, but also to help your children, your family and the people that you know, recognise that they too have permission to do same.

Give Yourself Permission to Succeed

Giving yourself permission is one of the 7 Underpinning Principles for living a happy, successful and fulfilling life. It plays such an important role in the quality of your life that it has its own section in this book.

Keep the Focus on Succeeding

What we focus on, greatly impacts on the way we think and operate. It governs the questions we ask and greatly affects our motivation and energy levels. In times of challenge, it is all too easy to focus heavily on worrying about survival and fear of failure. The problem is, this leaves us feeling fearful and disempowered. This, in turn, impedes the quality of our thinking, our emotional well-being and our capacity to take action.

The quality of our thinking has an enormous effect on our performance in every area of our lives. Olympic champions have absolute faith that they can win, they take consistent action to make winning a reality, and their focus over the years is often unwavering. Highly successful business people focus on achieving their vision; many of them have survived huge setbacks but have maintained their focus no matter what.

Be Self-Aware

Be aware of how you are operating. Think of a fly desperately flying into a window in the mindless effort of trying to get to the other side. Every time it buzzes and bumps into the window, it is using up its life force. No matter how frenzied the attempts become, the fly fails to reach its goal because it is trapped into repeating the same patterns of behaviour. It is so busy being busy (and buzzy) that it fails to notice the open door a couple of feet away.

The effort and struggle become part of the trap. Just like the fly, when you are engaged in huge amounts of busy-ness it is easy to lose sight of what is going on. It is so easy to get locked into a particular approach, so all you get is more struggle.

Determination by itself is never going to be enough. If you are expending lots of effort but feel you are getting nowhere, if you rely on the same thinking which is failing to get you the results you want, it is time to stop, take stock, and do something different. You need to shift your thinking, challenge your underpinning beliefs, and be prepared to get out of your comfort zone.

Create and Share Your Clear Vision for Success

Research has shown that the clearer you are about what you want to achieve, the easier it is to achieve it. It makes it easier to plan how to move from where you are to where you would like to be.

Foggy, vague wishes are really hard to implement. They lead to uncertainty, lots of delays, diversions, and dissatisfaction as it is difficult to determine how much progress is being made. We, humans, operate much more effectively when there is a plan to follow. Of course, the plan needs to be flexible; circumstances may change, but the plan helps you to keep things moving forward.

Creating a clear vision of the success you desire is an important step towards achieving your success as an individual. Having a vision of the desired success becomes even more important if achieving success involves others. That vision needs to be clear, explicit, shared and understood by all those involved. When everyone involved (partners, families, groups, movements, charities, schools, businesses) takes ownership of making the vision become a reality, success is so much easier to achieve and sustain.

You can find lots of practical help to support managers achieving success within a professional or organizational setting in my book 'Manage Your Staff More Effectively'.

If You Want to Achieve Success It Is Helpful to Ask Yourself the Following Questions:

- What specifically do I mean by 'success'?

If you are not able to define it you will never know if you have achieved it.

Why is it important to me? To others?

There is a huge body of evidence which shows that success is far more likely where those involved think their goal is important. When people are passionate about what they want to achieve, they are much less likely to be put off or to give up.

Define why your goal is important to you. If your goal involves others, get them on board too. You may think this is obvious, but I know from experience that individuals, teams, and whole organisations often spend a great deal of time and energy with little thought about why they are doing it. Levels of motivation and engagement rocket when everyone is on board with something they believe is right and will make a positive difference.

- **What would I need to see or experience to know that I have actually succeeded?**
- **What criteria will I use to measure my success?**

Criteria for measuring success may be based on achieving one specific goal–to meet my life partner, to have savings of over £100k, to feel healthy, to be debt-free, to get a promotion, to win an award for my business, to pass an exam, to write a book, to have a baby, to walk again, etc.

Your goal may be multi-layered and more complex, but knowing what needs to be in place, so you will know you have succeeded, is important. Growing your business, creating a successful organisation, and creating a reputation of excellence requires multiple activities, all of which need a defined set of criteria by which to measure progress and determine whether you have succeeded in achieving your ultimate goal.

- **How would achieving this success feel?**

What will it feel like for you on the day you succeed in achieving your goal? Allow yourself to experience just how great that will be. Imagine what you will do, how things will look and sound, and what difference that will make to your life and to others.

The more you are able to step into owning that success in advance, the more committed you will be. Your brain is incredible: Your thoughts become your reality. When you experience success in your imagination, the brain does its best to help you achieve your goal. Your thinking leads to choices, which then affect your behaviour, so you begin to operate in a different way. You begin to look for solutions rather than dwell on problems. Those of you familiar with the principle of manifestation will recognise this as a fundamental approach to achieving success. By itself, it will have limited impact, but when you combine imagining or visualising your success as it if has already happened with the other approaches outlined in this section, success is yours for the taking. Get in touch with the emotions your success engenders. The more real you make it, the more powerful the effect will be.

- **Who should I share my intention with?**

If you are truly committed to achieving your goal, let others know what you are doing and why.

Choose who you share with wisely. It can be helpful to sound out others when you are setting out to achieve a new goal. However, many people get put off before they even start because they share their ideas with people who are quick to squash both their ideas and enthusiasm. This is often done out of their fear and concern. They don't want you to be hurt or disappointed. The trouble is it has the potential to keep you stuck in your comfort zone, which acts as a straight-jacket.

There is a paradox. You have to determine whether the response from others is based on sound reasoning or not. If so, it is time to review your idea in the light of their feedback. If their warnings are based on fear and their own limitations, you have to decide whether to proceed or not.

You may find it useful to ask yourself the following questions:

- *What do I think underpins the advice the person has given me?* You need to be really honest with yourself and own your past decisions and behaviours. What is the evidence they are using to base their advice on? Do you have a history of starting things and giving up? Have you previously lost interest in your 'latest project'? Do you make a habit of doing so?

- *If I go ahead–what is the likely impact on others if I fail, or if I succeed?*
- *Why do I want to do this–what's my **real** motive?*
- *How important to me is it that I achieve success in **this** particular way?*
- *How will I feel if I give this **goal** up?*
- *How determined am I that I **will** make this work?* Score it out of 10, where 1 is 'not bothered at all', and 10 is 'nothing will get in my way'.
- *Am I ready to take ownership for making this happen?*

Ready? Then It's Action Time. Here's What to Do

- **What do I need to do?**

Once you state your intention to achieve something, it takes on a reality that is quite different from the one you keep secret in your head. Defining your goal and making a public declaration of your intention does a number of things:

- It sends a strong, energetic message that you mean business, no more sitting on the fence.
- It deepens your commitment to taking sustained action.
- It allows other people to hold you to account.

- **Who else needs to be involved?**
- **Who will be cheering me on?**

Identifying the right people who will act as your mentors, cheerleaders, advocates, and supporters can increase your chances of success enormously. Creating a team of people prepared to offer support, encouragement, advice, and practical help is enormously helpful. Having others who have faith in your capacity to succeed, especially in those dark moments of doubt and challenge, can make all the difference. That is when working with a coach and having the support of a positive peer group like the Thrive Together Tribe can help.

Model those who have already succeeded in your field. Engage the services of a coach or mentor.

- **Is my goal personal or does it involve others?**

The more people who are actively involved in making your success a reality, the more important it will be to have a defined vision and a strategic plan or roadmap for how you intend to achieve it. Just as important is clear, shared, ongoing effective communication.

I am amazed at how few people know what exactly they are aiming for. There is little or no strategic planning, so time, energy, and money are wasted. It is like getting your car out of the garage and driving to some vague destination (for example, 'some place pleasant') with no idea of how to get there or what exactly constitutes that place. It is then impossible to decide if you have actually arrived because there are no points of reference.

Once you know what you are aiming for, it is so much easier to plan the journey step by step. Planning needs to be structured rather than rigid; strategic planning is vital to ensure that you maximise the use of your time, energy, finances, and the resources that are at your disposal. Breaking things down into bite-size pieces avoids your being overwhelmed. After all, you wouldn't attempt to eat a whole cow or a field of corn in a single sitting; however, it is reasonable and enjoyable to do so bite by bite, meal by meal.

Strategic plans work best if you include a clear destination, milestones for measuring progress, costs, as it is so easy for lack of finance to scupper even the best ideas, a timeframe, and contingency plans in case things go off-track. You will find a prompt sheet at https://genuinely-you.com and lots of great information and practical strategies to manage others in 'How To Manage Your Staff More Effectively', including creating a strategic vision, effective team building, delegating effectively, and holding people to account.

This may sound rather business-oriented, but the principles are just as important for goals like getting healthy and losing weight, giving up smoking, finding your soul mate, living abroad for a year, or fulfilling your bucket list, as they are in completing a big project at work.

I have been surprised at how often clients who manage complex projects at work fail to transfer the same skills into their personal lives.

- **What action do I need to take and when?**

Your success will depend on your taking sustained action. Your approach to action will determine whether you fail or succeed. Many people go for the grand gesture, the huge one-off action, which is unsustainable and is never followed through.

A simple example is those who create a New Year's resolution to get fit. They buy all the right gear, join a flashy gym, and on the first of January arrive at the gym, determined to make it work. They work out for an hour and a half, try every machine, and end up exhausted, in pain, and barely able to walk. After taking several days to recover, the thought of going back to the gym fills them with dread, so they put it off, make excuses, and head for the tin of biscuits. It is a common but highly dubious way of achieving success.

Highly successful people do things very differently. Their actions are sustained on a daily basis over time. It is small actions sustained over time, which make the real difference to achieving success. Highly successful people take some action towards their goal every single day. For example, successful people, who've made it a priority to live healthy, exercise several days a week, even when the weather is bad, when they feel tired, or when there are other more interesting things to do. They keep their focus on the goal of overall good health and fitness. They are regular and consistent with their exercise. That way, they achieve and maintain their goal.

Kiss the Frog

Very successful people will do things they don't enjoy, even things they hate doing if it will help them achieve the success they desire. They will also regularly get on and do the things they dislike first. Less successful people would rather give up on their dreams of success than face doing things they don't like doing or which make them feel uncomfortable.

Doing the stuff you don't like doing first, makes a huge difference. It is so easy to find distractions or allow interruptions to become an excuse for not getting on with the difficult tasks. Avoidance becomes procrastination, the biggest enemy of creating sustained success.

One really useful strategy is 'kissing the frog'. Here is how it works:

When we have incompletions–things we know we should, need, and ought to do, but we find difficulty–it is really common to keep putting the job at the bottom of the to-do list. I know how easy it is to what I call 'faff about' or 'fiddle about' with lots of things that don't really matter as a distraction from the job I don't want to do. However, avoiding the difficult jobs leaches your energy. The incompletions take on a bigger and bigger space in your thoughts, and as they do, they take on an energy of their own. Their magnitude expands until they leave you feeling powerless and impotent. They lead to procrastination and eventually to becoming totally stuck.

When you 'kiss the frog', you get the most challenging job done at the beginning of the day. Not only does it get the nasty stuff out of the way, but it creates a sense of achievement, a positive momentum which carries the day forward in a far more positive way.

Let me give you some examples:

I was talking with a client who needed to create the copy for her website. Her business was in limbo because of the delay caused by her failure to meet deadline after deadline. An even bigger issue was the impact on her sense of wellbeing and confidence. The more she delayed and found excuses not to get started, the bigger the challenge seemed to be, and we already know how powerful the mind is at making that which 'seems' into that which 'is' . . .The more she feared failure and did nothing, the more likely her business was to fail. The suggestion of buying the services of a professional copywriter was dismissed out of hand by her because she felt that would mean she had failed. She was stressed, unhappy, and stuck!

The solution:

We planned how she would tackle the task; we broke it down into small bite-size chunks and created a timetable for achieving what was required. Once the detailed plan was created, she agreed to kiss the frog, which involved sitting down to write for 15 minutes each morning before doing anything else. Initially, my client found it a challenge, but she did it. After a very short time, she began to see progress and found it easier to work at the task for longer. Within a couple of weeks, she found a rhythm which meant that the copy was finished well within the timeframe we'd planned.

On a personal note:

I started to do Facebook live videos a few weeks ago. I felt uncomfortable about being live on camera as I had never done it before. I felt vulnerable and exposed. For several weeks, I fiddled around doing other things; days went by and the whole time at the back of my mind was the niggling thought that I still hadn't done what I needed to do.

Two weeks ago, I finally took myself in hand. I was at a networking meeting where it is traditional to declare our goals for the next month, and I publicly declared my goal to the group: to create at least twenty Facebook live videos before the next meeting. I am on track! I have now done ten. I am finding it easier and easier, and know I will get all twenty done before the next meeting. I should add that it is much easier to kiss the frog when you declare it as a goal before other people!

Your Expectations

Of Yourself?

You never really know what you are capable of until you put it to the test. How often have you watched or read the news when someone has done something out of the ordinary? I believe we are all capable of extraordinary things: You only need to look at what happens in times of extreme challenge. I also believe that we can be extraordinary without the need of war, tragedy, or emergency. When you step into the power of being your genuine best self, you are capable of living an extraordinary life, one of endless possibilities.

Of Timescales?

As noted earlier in the book, it is really common to overestimate what we can do in a day or a week but to underestimate what we can do over a month or a year. Success requires sustained action.

For Avoiding Potential Pitfalls?

Don't Get Stuck in the Quicksand of 'Trying'

How often have you heard the saying, 'If at first, you don't succeed, try, try, try again'? I know I must have said it thousands of times when I was in teaching. Trying to do something and doing something are two very different things. When I try to move something forward, the try stops exactly at the point of moving. The try part of the activity has no movement, no action, no chance of success. Success is based on taking whatever action is necessary to move forward, rather than staying stuck in the limbo of 'try'. I wish I had recognized this distinction earlier, but I had not yet realised that trying can all too easily keep you stuck. Trying is just like quicksand: It seems safe enough, but it can kill any chance of sustained success.

Now the advice I give is very different: Either choose to do it or not to do it. Trying is a cop out. The danger is that trying gives you an excuse not to push through and take real action. Taking action, being prepared to fail, learning from those failed attempts, and taking action again until you find what works is the best approach. It leads to sustained success!

Find an object, something like a pen, mug, or cushion. Try to move it. I'm sure you will have succeeded, but in the actual move you are no longer trying; you are taking action, you are moving it. The instant you start to create any momentum you have moved from 'try' into 'act'.

How often do you use the 'I am trying' excuse?

If you want to succeed and are stuck in the 'trying' quicksand, it is important to get out of that habit, to ensure that you are determined to move forward, to make a change, and to take action.

When Your Comfort Zone Becomes a Straight-Jacket

Your comfort zone is where you feel at home. You feel confident and perfectly safe within your comfort zone. Comfort zones are absolutely tailored to each individual; they are based on your previous experiences and your beliefs.

We all need some level of certainty and security. We will do anything to ensure that our need for certainty is satisfied. It is important to recognise that each of us will have our own particular version of what certainty looks like. If we had total certainty, it would be like living a 'groundhog day' life (like in the movie?). Life would be boring if we had no level of variety or challenge.

It is the balance between our need for certainty and security, and our capacity to deal with variety and uncertainty that determines how confined or expansive our comfort zone will be. There is nothing good or bad about where the balance lies between your need for routine and structure, and the level of spontaneity, surprise, and adventure you need in your life. They are simply different.

Understanding what motivates you and others in your life is incredibly useful. You will find a complete model of motivation in Chapter 7 Secret Pathway 4–Choice.

When you are surrounded by what is familiar, doing the activities you know you can achieve with ease, your comfort zone remains exactly as it is. Growth comes out of challenge. Unless we are confronted by something different, nothing will change. Our unconscious mind has one major purpose–to ensure we survive. It is entirely risk-averse. Your unconscious mind will identify all the reasons why it is not a good idea to do something unfamiliar. The greater your need for certainty, the more you will choose to stay within your comfort zone.

A comfort zone is like a duvet, a great, big, thick, fluffy, duvet. In the winter, it's lovely to wrap yourself up in the duvet and feel comfortable and warm. But on a very hot day, if I were to wrap myself in that duvet, it would feel constricting and smothering. When you stay within your comfort zone, it feels safe and cosy and warm initially; however, when you stay stuck in your comfort zone, it begins to limit your world. It makes the world smaller and smaller, making life feel constricted, so you begin to feel smothered. Your choices become more and more limited.

The strange thing is that your comfort zone may keep you stuck in situations that are the complete opposite of comfortable. Many people stay stuck in the most awful circumstances: abusive relationships, loveless marriages, hated jobs. Why? Because making the changes necessary to create a new, more empowering life would require them to step outside their comfort zone. They would need to enter the unknown. So they work on the basis of 'better the devil you know'; they avoid 'stepping out of the frying pan into the fire'. In doing so, they stay stuck in a place of pain and limitation.

Crossing the Line of Perturbation

The line of perturbation is at the boundary between your comfort zone and facing your fear when you do something different.

The line of perturbation is that point where your comfort zone meets something new. It is common for people to repeatedly get to the line of perturbation but give up before going across into new territory. As soon as you cross the line of perturbation, the boundary expands, and the line of perturbation moves forward, expanding your range of comfort. Once your comfort zone expands, the thing you felt so nervous about, because it was new and unfamiliar, becomes less scary. The more you repeat the activity, the easier it becomes; the more it sits within your newly-expanded comfort zone. It is how you learn and grow.

CROSSING THE LINE OF PERTUBATION

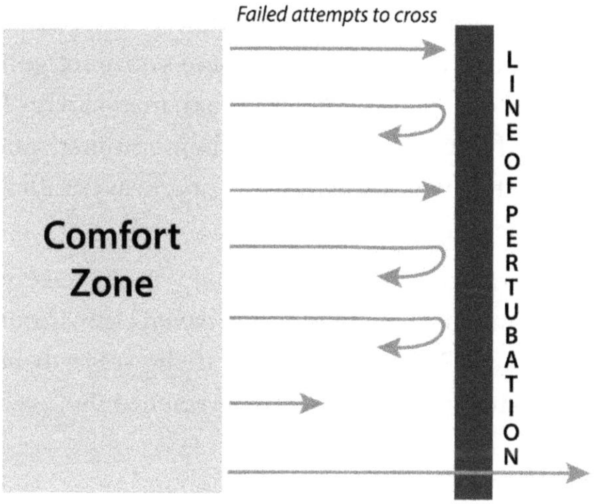

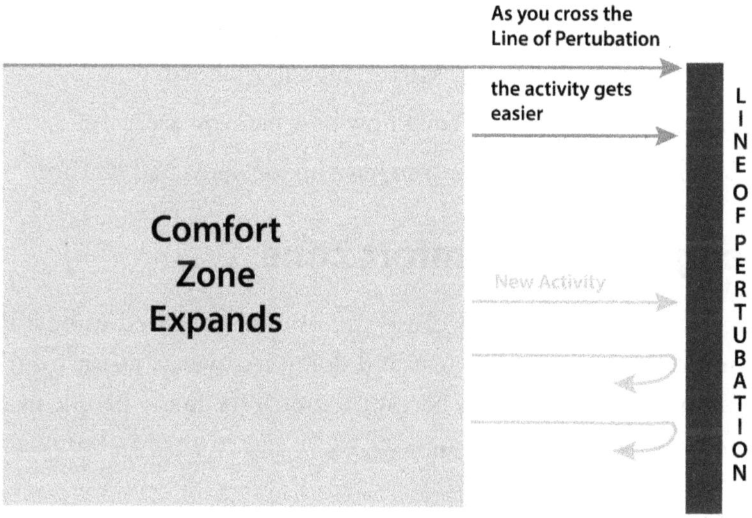

The more you do the action which initially made you anxious, the more comfort you will feel.

Let me give you an example: learning to drive. Think about the first time you got behind the wheel of a car. How nervous were you? How difficult did you find it to coordinate the accelerator, brakes, and clutch? To steer and watch the road and remember where you were going? Do you remember learning the sequence: mirror, signal, manoeuvre? I expect you felt very much out of your comfort zone when you first started dealing with the mechanics of driving the car, managing heavy traffic and having to remember all of the rules of the road.

I ask you as an experienced driver, 'How many times have you actually arrived at your destination and found you haven't consciously thought about your driving at all?' You have reached the stage of being totally comfortable about driving your car; you have reached the level of mastery.

The Four Levels of Competence

- *Unconscious Competence / Mastery:* You do things well without having to think about it consciously. It has become an unconscious act which comes naturally.
- *Conscious Competence:* You know you can do it but you have to think about it consciously. E.g. Mirror, Signal, Manoeuvre.
- *Conscious Incompetence:* You know how bad you are.
- *Unconscious Incompetence:* You have no idea how bad you are.

Challenging Your Comfort Zone

How often do you stay stuck because you are not prepared to be a little bit uncomfortable? Feeling the fear and doing it anyway, taken from the title of Susan Jeffers's book, has become a motto for many people in self-development. It's an important message we've visited already, but one that is so important it is worth revisiting.

Everyone feels fearful at times. Successful people are no different. The difference is that successful people go for it. When they attempt something but don't succeed, they simply give it another go. They learn to make adjustments as they go. The process of learning from failures is a vital factor in creating ongoing success. Failing to have a go and-or failing to learn from an experience are the only true failures.

My comfort zone has been incredibly stretched by all the new technology I have had to use in developing the Thrive Together Tribe. I'm very good at the things I have learned to do over the almost-40 years of my professional life. Public speaking, training, coaching, consulting, teaching, and running groups all feel familiar, but I have found that I have been hugely out of my comfort zone over the past few months, wrestling with new technology. Even so, I am not going to let that stop me from moving forward. To achieve my goal, I have to become confident in using a wide range of different pieces of software; I have to learn new techniques and how to use unfamiliar technology. I've had a few significant setbacks because all of these things are new and challenging. However, the more I practise these things, the easier they are becoming. As I gain confidence, as my comfort zone expands, everything is feeling easier. It will be the same for you.

Let me add: There is a difference between trying and practising something to gain mastery of it. Practice is a specific action with an outcome. Trying is simply an intention until the direct action begins. When you find yourself trying but getting nowhere, making no evaluation of your failed attempts in order to make the success of further action more likely, then consider whether you have become caught up in the 'trying' quicksand.

Be Aware of Your Internal Chatter

Internal chatter is that voice that goes on and on in your head, urging and cajoling, 'You should have done this, you shouldn't have done that, you must, you mustn't, why did you? why didn't you? . . . '.

The critical voice that nags on and on, can be incredibly destructive. How often do you have that voice in your head? Does it simply keep you on track in a benign way, or is it being destructively critical? Whose voice is it? Is it yours? Or is it the voice of a parent or a teacher telling you that you're not good enough? If it is a ghost of the past, give yourself permission to tell it to shut up. Your own voice has far more power than the opinion of others to build you up or to be destructive.

It's important to recognise the difference between the voice which encourages you to do well and to do it properly, and the voice which constantly nags. If you find your chatter telling you over and over again that you didn't do it properly, that it is never going to be good enough, then it is time to change the message. The chatter is not achieving anything other than making you feel bad. It is time to praise yourself, to acknowledge your achievements, and to install empowering, positive messages: 'I am good enough, I can do this, I am an amazing, powerful person, I choose to be happy and successful!'

Think of the impact this chatter is having on your sense of possibilities. The language we use is incredibly powerful; remember the connecting theme of the power of language.

Wasting Your Resources

It is important to remember you only have three personal resources at your disposal: time, energy, and money. They are finite resources. How much of them you have and how you use them, is up to you. Once you have used them, they are gone, so it makes sense to use them wisely. How you choose to spend each of these precious resources makes a huge difference to the quality of life you lead and the level of success you experience.

Time

Minute by minute you choose what you do with your time. You may choose not to make a conscious choice and allow time to drift, or you may have a carefully set up schedule for four every day of the week. When considering time and success, one of the most common excuses people use for not succeeding is lack of time.

A professor was giving a lecture. He showed his students a large glass jar. He took a bag of stones, each about the size of a tennis ball, and put them in the jar. He asked the class if the jar was full. They agreed it was.

He then took a bag of pebbles and began to fill the spaces between the stones with them. He asked again if the jar was full. His students replied that it was.

The professor then took a bag of sand and water and filled the jar to the brim.

He explained the stones represented the important things in life: family, health, dreams, and aspirations. The pebbles represented things that were less important: job, house, and car. The sand and water represented the least important things: running errands, watching TV, worrying, complaining. He then asked his students to consider how the life represented by the full jar would be if it had been filled with sand and water first. The response: There would have been no room left for the pebbles or stones, i.e., the most and second most important things in a person's life.

The lesson: Be particular with how you fill your glass jar–be careful how you choose to spend your time over the course of your life.

There are 24 hours in every day, 168 hours in a week, 8,736 hours in a year, and 613,200 hours in a life of seventy years. By the time you take out time for sleeping, working, including the travel to and from work, preparing and eating food, keeping clean, and so on, it is easy to see how time slips away.

How do you spend your time currently? Do you value your time enough to use it wisely?

We never know how much time we have on this earth, so it makes sense not to waste it.

Please don't think that I mean you have to be busy all the time. Indeed I'm saying something very different. Are you so busy that you are completely oblivious to the magical things around you? Do you make time for the people who really matter to you? Are you a human being or a human doing? Do you find yourself spending a lot of time doing stuff that doesn't really matter? How much time do you spend wishing things were different, complaining about things, or listening to others moan? None of these things add value to your life, and they certainly don't contribute to your success. In fact, these are the things that make you feel drained and tired.

What do you value enough to spend your time on? Be mindful about how you use your time and make it count. Sitting quietly and noticing the beauty around you has huge value. Learn to be productive rather than busy.

The Dalai Lama said, 'There are only two days a year that nothing can be done. One is called yesterday and the other is called tomorrow. Today is the right day to love, believe, do, and mostly, live'. Yet, many people spend a significant proportion of their time focusing on what has happened in the past; others spend most of their time on worrying about the future. In both cases they miss out on the journey; they fail to live in the present moment and miss so much as a result.

Are you making the most of your time?

Imagine you are at the end of your life looking back through time. Look back over those years and consider how you would like to be remembered. What legacy would you like to leave?

Imagine you are creating a eulogy for the person who is you as you live your life now. How would that eulogy go if you had lived your ideal life?

What needs to change?

Managing time is about prioritising and making choices. To do that effectively will often require you to create boundaries, to learn to say no–to others and maybe to yourself when it is appropriate to do so.

Even a small change can make a significant difference to the quality of your life and to your success. For example, Kathryn came to see me because she was feeling overwhelmed. As a single working parent, she spent her entire life juggling and chasing her tail. Her to-do list was monumental, and as a result, Kathryn felt she was failing her children and her colleagues. She felt awful.

We tackled the problem in a number of ways:

Her children were ages 9 and 11. Up until that point, the children had done nothing to help around the house. Kathryn spent all her time racing around trying to do everything, so there was no time left for them to spend time doing family things. Kathryn implemented a family conference where tasks appropriate to the children's age and ability were agreed on. In return, they set up family time where she and the children took it in turns to choose the activity. For the first time in a very long time, the children were able to spend some time with their mum where her attention was not on the chores that needed to be done. Kathryn felt better about things, and the children were much happier.

Kathryn's to-do list had no system for prioritising what was both urgent and important. Everything was simply plonked on the list, thus making it difficult to see the wood for the trees. I suggested a simple way to prioritise her list to make it more manageable:

At the end of each day, (for the following day), go through your to-do list and mark each one in the following way:

A = It must be done today. It is both urgent and important.

B = It needs to be done, ideally today if there is time after all the As have been completed. If not, it will be an A tomorrow.

C = This can wait, but I need to keep an eye on the timing, so I can upgrade it to a B or an A in the future.

D = This needs to be done, but it doesn't need to be me. I can delegate this. I must put a note to monitor progress at the appropriate time.

We also discussed ways Kathryn would manage things at work when there was too much to do in too little time. Helping her feel she could be assertive was an important part of this. Having the confidence to be assertive is very closely aligned with a positive sense of self-worth. She learned to talk to her boss differently: 'You have asked me to do X. I'm happy to do it, but it will mean leaving something else until later, as there simply isn't time to complete it all in the timescale available. Can we go through my to-do list, so I can be sure I know what your priorities are, please?'

Any one of these changes has the capacity to make a difference. Collectively they made a significant difference to Kathryn.

The Thrive Together Tribe Resource Bank has lots of time-saving strategies for you to dip into.

What change/s could you make today that would make a positive difference to the quality of your life over time?

Energy

It is so easy to take your energy for granted until it is in short supply. I know that from personal experience. Fatigue and lack of energy are consistent challenges for me. The gift in this is that I have learned (the hard way) to have a huge regard for how I spend my energy. I look for smart ways to achieve my goal, and I am far less prepared to squander what energy I have.

If you want to feel vital and full of energy, it is imperative that you look after your body. It isn't rocket science: Nourishing food will give you more energy than eating lots of high fat, high salt, and-or sugary foods. Drinking plenty of water is important too, as is getting enough sleep. Avoiding the things which are known to impact your health negatively, such as smoking, too much alcohol, caffeine, or sugar, or taking recreational drugs, will help you feel more energised. If you know your diet and lifestyle are getting in the way of your feeling great, you can choose to carry on being destructive or to make the changes that will enhance your levels of available energy.

Emotional Energy

Your emotional wellbeing has a direct and profound impact on your level of physical energy. Negative emotions leech your energy, leaving you exhausted and un-resourced. Worrying about things, especially those things which may never happen, takes huge amounts of energy for very little return. Depression and anxiety have an enormous effect on how much energy is available for other things. Holding onto old hurts and regrets is also expensive in terms of your energy. Positive emotions energise you and provide a sense of possibility. It is far easier to access your personal resources from a positive emotional state. Gratitude, doing things you are passionate about, and being playful in your approach will create greatly increased levels of energy.

Laughter is incredibly energising. It releases the feel-good hormones: endorphins, dopamine, and serotonin. The feel-good hormones form one of the two biggest antidotes to stress; the other being exercise. Both activities help the body to deal with the hormones we create when we are under stress: adrenaline, hydrocortisone, and cortisol.

Knowing that your state of mind has such an impact on your levels of energy is only the first step. What then?

You'll find lots of things to help deal with negative emotions on the Genuinely You website https://genuinely-you.com

The Personal Empowerment Plan (PEP talks) is a six-month programme designed to help you deal effectively with stress and anxiety. That is also available on the website.

Many people find it difficult to share things when they feel unhappy or worried. They may not want to burden friends and family or feel that family, friends, or colleagues will be judgemental if they admit they need help. The Thrive Together Tribe can help by providing you with a forum that is both non-judgemental and supportive.

Dealing with negative feelings can feel overwhelming, so I've included some simple processes which really help when you use them regularly.

An Exercise in Mindfulness

This 3- to 5-minute exercise is really helpful for preventing and managing stress and anxiety. Here's how it works:

Find a quiet place.

Take 4 deep breaths. Breathe in through your nose and out through your mouth. Breathe in deeply, and as you do, imagine you are breathing all the way down to your toes.

Give yourself permission to breathe out all the negative feelings and to breathe in calm white light.

Close your eyes.

Concentrate only on what you can hear. Be aware of all the sounds you can hear. Allow yourself to settle and hear the smallest sounds in the distance. Be aware of the sound of your own breathing.

Now concentrate on what you can feel: the fabric of your clothes on your skin, the pressure on the back of your thighs as they press on the chair, any movement of air from the air conditioning or a breeze through the window; take note of everything you can feel.

Change your concentration onto what you can smell. Are you wearing aftershave or perfume? Can you smell polish or any chemical smell? What about the smell of food in the air?

What can you taste? Have you recently had a coffee or eaten a mint? Take a moment to notice.

Lastly–open your eyes. Without swivelling your head, what can you see? Look at the colours, textures, and shapes you can see. How is the light playing in the room? Are there any bright spots or shadows?

Allow yourself to come back to the present.

This technique is great for keeping stress at bay. Doing it three or four times a day can make a huge difference. It is also incredibly helpful if you are feeling anxious or stressed, as a way of regaining your equilibrium.

Two Exercises for Dealing with Negative Emotion

If you try to ignore negative emotions or bury them, they have a nasty habit of coming back stronger, often at the most inconvenient times. Research has shown that when they persist over time, they have a detrimental impact on your health, particularly your immune system. They certainly have the potential to derail your mood and so much more. Negative emotions leave you feeling awful. It becomes difficult to access your personal resources–

confidence, courage, calmness, positivity, optimism, resilience, the ability to see solutions, and so on.

Many clients I've worked with have been too frightened to confront their negative emotions. They have buried them deep or anaesthetised themselves with food, alcohol, or drugs etc. They have used smoking or shopping to help them dampen down the pain created by ignoring their negative emotions and the issues which have created them.

It is important to look for the underlying lesson within the negative emotion. If you don't deal with what is causing the issue, it will continue to be a challenge until you do so. The emotion may ease for a while, but it will return, and will often feel more and more difficult to deal with. In my experience, until you grasp the nettle, you will continue to meet challenges designed to help you recognise there is a lesson to be learned. Those challenges often get bigger and bigger until we can no longer ignore them.

Confronting the issue may feel overwhelming at the start. Getting professional help can be really helpful, as is having a supportive peer group. I've worked with clients who have suffered the most horrendous abuse and those who have dealt with enormous challenges and injustice. They have one thing in common: They were trapped in past hurts until they were prepared to confront the problem–the 'dragon in the box'–and deal with it. Only then were they able to let go of the past, enjoy the present, and look forward to a future where they could appreciate the endless possibilities it offered.

The following processes have been found to be really helpful in making negative emotions feel more manageable. Do these exercises in a quiet place with your eyes closed.

Option One: Connecting with the Earth's Centre

1. Take three deep breaths.
2. Scan your body from the top of your head right down to your toes.
3. Which emotions are you feeling?

4. Where in your body are you feeling that emotion? Is it in your throat, in your solar plexus, around your shoulders? It could be located anywhere.
5. Imagine that you have a deep round pipe going from the very bottom of your spine right into the centre of the Earth.
6. Give yourself permission to send that negative emotion down the pipe, right down into the centre of the Earth.
7. Think about which positive emotion you would like to replace the negative emotion. Every negative emotion has a positive counterpart: fear–courage; anxiety–calm; sadness–happiness, etc. Choose the positive emotions which would work best for you; there are no right or wrong answers.
8. Send the negative emotion down the pipe to the centre of the Earth. As it reaches the centre of the Earth, imagine the pressure is transforming it into the positive energy you have just identified. Imagine the positive emotion you have chosen is now flooding into the space that has been left by negative emotion. Don't worry if you are not good at visualising. Give yourself permission to imagine.

Option Two: Wash It Away

1. Identify the negative emotion which you want to work with, and give yourself permission to let go of it.
2. Imagine yourself floating in a beautiful tropical lake. The lake is idyllic; there is no threat of anything that could hurt you.
3. The lake is surrounded by lush gardens or woods. Use each of your senses to make the scene come alive. What can you see, hear, feel, smell, and taste? The more you fill in the details, the better this works.
4. Imagine that at one end of the lake is a beautiful waterfall. The water is catching the light, glistening as it falls into the lake.

5. At the other end of the lake are large, powerful magnets. The lake is like an infinity pool, from just behind the magnets, the water cascades down into a river below.
6. Go and stand under the waterfall. Let the gentle flow of water wash out the negative emotion. Imagine the magnets are drawing out the negative emotion from the water around you. It is pulled to the edge of the lake and then falls over the edge into the river below. The magnets are as powerful as you need them to be to draw out the negativity.
7. Ask your unconscious mind to let the negative emotion go, to allow the body to reset to perfect factory settings.
8. If you feel resistance to letting go of the emotion, imagine a large film screen (just like an outdoor cinema screen) in front of you. Put a symbol to represent the block to letting go of the negative emotion up onto that screen.
9. Send the block to the magnet. If that doesn't work, put up another screen in front of the first. Create another symbol to represent the block to the block. Let the magnet draw the negative emotion across the lake and over the edge of the river below.
10. If that still doesn't work, keep creating screens with symbols to represent the block to the block to the block. Eventually, the unconscious mind will give up. It will finally release the negative emotion so it can be drawn to the magnets.
11. Allow the water from the waterfall to fill the space left by losing the negative emotion with healing light, hope, and a sense of endless possibilities. Choose colours and positive emotions to fill you up.

This exercise works really well if you have emotional or physical pain such as a backache, headache or period pains. Allow the water to wash away the pain.

Money

Money is really just another form of energy, the currency of exchange. Your beliefs underpin the relationship you have with money. I've covered this in some detail in chapter 4 Secret Pathway 1–Belief. Having a positive, healthy relationship with money is vital if you want to enjoy financial freedom. It is imperative that you take responsibility for your financial situation. Understanding the difference between good debt and bad debt is important if you are to make the best out of the money available to you.

Good vs. Bad Debt

A good debt is an investment in something which will grow in value over time. Property is often considered to be the best example. Investing in art, jewellery, wine, etc. requires a level of expertise and a significant tolerance to risk.

Investing in stocks, shares, commodities, and unit trusts have created many people a sizable fortune. Many have also been caught by a falling market and lost large amounts of money.

Whatever you invest in, do it mindfully. Take advice from a variety of sources and trust your gut feeling. If a deal sounds too good to be true, it probably is.

Investing in the tools of your trade and the learning to help you use them are worthwhile expenses as they are investments for the future.

Highly successful people are prepared to delay gratification in order to achieve their long-term goals. Some long-term research into deferred gratification has been done with very young children. The initial stage of the 'marshmallow experiment' took place with a group of pre-schoolers aged around 3 to 4. Each child was placed in a room on their own. In the room was a plate with a marshmallow on it. They were told not to eat the sweets. If they waited until the adult returned to the room, they could then have two marshmallows. The room was fitted with a two-way observational mirror. Some children were happy to wait until the return of the researcher. Some employed distraction techniques to help them withstand the temptation. Others were unable to withstand the temptation and ate the sweet before the researcher returned.

The interesting part of the research came as the same children were tracked over the decades, well into adulthood. The results were stark. The children who gave into temptation continued to find difficulty in deferred gratification; as adults, they were fatter, professionally less successful, and had accrued far greater levels of debt. The children who had the capacity to defer gratification early in life were fitter, financially better off, and had achieved significantly greater success. There is a strong message here for parents: Giving into your child's every wish as they grow up could be damaging to their long-term future. Experiencing the satisfaction of working towards a goal and succeeding over time is an incredibly enriching learning experience.

Bad debt is an investment which will decline in value or which has no capacity to grow value. Most cars depreciate, holidays are lovely but are not an investment. Clothes, jewellery, eating out, drinks, cigarettes, and even buying coffee can quickly result in mounting debt unless you keep track of your spending.

I have been surprised at how common it is for clients to become very efficient ostriches when it comes to debt. Credit cards are very useful, but unless you pay them off in full every month, they are costing you a fortune in compound interest. The interest charged by banks racks up really quickly if you are paying off only the minimum repayment.

I was working with a client called Sue. She came to me initially because of her high levels of stress. It wasn't long before her financial status became clear. She was in over £50,000 of debt, none of which was related to college or university fees. Together we mapped out where her money was going. Sue was in employment, earned a good salary, and her expenses and mortgage should have been very manageable.

I'll just pick out a few of the things we identified:

Each month her debt was increasing by a hefty amount as she was only paying the minimum amount off her credit card bill. Sue smoked 30 cigarettes a day at the cost of £7.50 per packet or around £2,740 per year. She drank a bottle of wine a day at the cost of around £7 per bottle, which meant £2,555 per year. She bought a cappuccino and roll on the way to work every work-day morning, costing £6 per day. This mounted up to £1,440 over the year. She always bought lunch out during the working week; this ranged from a sandwich and a drink to a pub meal on Friday. We costed this out at least £2,000 over the year. When Sue felt fed up (which was quite often), she would go and buy something to cheer herself up, a pair of shoes, an outfit, or a handbag. Her taste was not cheap. She didn't like cooking but loved entertaining, so she bought lots of convenience foods with a high price tag.

You can see how her debts had mounted. She was living well above her means, and she is not alone.

We created a debt eradication plan for Sue, which included reducing her smoking and consumption of wine, and making her breakfast and lunch at home. These changes saved a significant amount of money across the month. Buying things to improve her mood was replaced by using the strategies she learned within our sessions.

All of the money saved was used to offset her debt. Because she began to live within her means, Sue was no longer adding to the debt each month. Taking control of her life had a really positive impact on how she felt about herself. That, in turn, helped her manage and sustain all the changes. Sue began to enjoy cooking and being inventive with food. Her mood, energy levels, and general health all improved because of the improvement in diet and the reduction of alcohol and nicotine.

Repaying the debt was done in a very specific way. Sue was unable to transfer the debt to another credit card with a period of interest-free time. (This can be a good way to manage your debt, but only if you repay the debt before the prescribed period ends.) Sue had 6 credit cards, and each had a different rate of interest. She continued to pay the minimum repayment on 5 of the cards and used any spare cash at the end of the month, to pay off the card with the highest rate of interest first. Once that was paid off, she then took each card, in turn, always paying off the one with the highest interest.

After a few weeks, Sue really got the bit between her teeth. She began to look for ways to pay off the debt more quickly. She sold lots of clothes, shoes, and handbags on eBay. Many of which she had hardly worn. Some still had the labels on. She started a part-time job in a bar in the evenings, which she really enjoyed because she met lots of new people. Within two years, she was debt-free, much healthier, and much happier.

Investing in Yourself

Investing in yourself is important, but don't kid yourself into thinking that buying yet another handbag, a pair of shoes, or a flash new car counts, as they are not a sound investment.

Education, self-development courses, books, etc., are great investments if and only if–you do something with them. I've met lots of people who have spent thousands of pounds on courses but have changed nothing as a result. Sadly, they have convinced themselves that attending the course is the magic bullet. The reality is the course, the book, the video, all have the capacity to be the catalysts for change. The only thing which will have any lasting impact on your life is if you take responsibility for your life and consistently act to change it.

Investing in good grooming doesn't have to cost a great deal, but it has a significant impact on your confidence. Clothes don't have to be expensive to look good; the important thing is to make sure you feel groomed and dressed appropriately for each situation.

Use Your Money to Buy the Time and Energy of Others

Whether to do it yourself or to pay for others to do tasks you are no good at or don't have time to do is a question, which many people find difficult to decide, particularly when they are on a tight budget.

Here are the principles I've used which I've found to be really helpful.

I am happy to pay for another's expertise. I use it to educate and train myself if it is a skill I will need on a regular basis. If it is a skill which will be needed just for now or for something which will only be needed occasionally, I will buy in the expertise to do the job itself.

Let me give you an example. When I was a head teacher, we had to do the closedown of one financial year and set the new financial year up on the computer. It was by its very nature an annual event. It was complex, and it was important that we got it right, or it could cause endless problems for us and the local authority throughout the year. I decided to buy in expert help to do it. They were able to do it in a fraction of the time I and my office staff would have needed. They had an absolute knowledge of the process and enough experience to deal with any technical problem the process threw up.

I know I work best when I'm doing something I'm really passionate about. Whenever possible, I have chosen to buy the time of others to do the things which bore the pants off me. I look for people who are passionate about doing the very things I hate. My time is then more productively (and pleasantly) used in earning the money to pay them.

As fatigue is an ongoing problem for me, one of my priorities is to buy help for the physically challenging things which would completely incapacitate me if I were to do them: ironing, house cleaning, heavy gardening, etc.

Modelling Those Who Have Already Succeeded

It makes no sense to reinvent the wheel, but I know from clients that this is an incredibly common approach. To achieve your success more quickly and efficiently, look for others who have trodden the path successfully before. Learn from their mistakes and share in the approach they used to create their success. This principle is at the heart of this book and the Thrive Together Tribe.

The arrival of the internet has made this a whole lot easier. It is amazing what you can find on iTunes, podcasts, and YouTube. However, be warned: You have to be very aware that just because it is on the internet, doesn't mean it is either true or appropriate for you. Use your judgement. Remember, it is very easy to get sucked into watching endless stuff and think you are making progress when in the real sense you are not. It can very easily become another distraction or form of procrastination dressed up in the guise of being helpful. Watching and listening have their place, but success requires sustained activity.

Ask for Help

Accessing the expertise and experience of others can save you an enormous amount of time, money, and aggravation.

Dream Big

When I was in primary school, they adopted Douglas Barder's (RAF WW2 hero) motto, 'Aim for the stars'. It has stayed with me and proved to be a valuable approach to life. If you shoot for the stars and hit the moon, that's OK, but you have to shoot for something! A lot of people don't even shoot.

There are so many examples of people who have achieved seemingly impossible dreams: the Wright brothers who had the determination and faith to fly; Steve Jobs who dreamt of having a computer in the hands of everyday people. When they created their dreams, they initially had no idea of how to achieve their goals; they just dreamed big and then worked out the plan of how to create their success. They engaged in sustained action until they succeeded.

Needing to know the nuts and bolts of how to achieve success before starting, has stopped many people from doing anything. Have the dream and allow the 'how' to evolve. When you have the dream, the determination, and the persistence, nothing can get in the way of your success.

Oprah Winfrey offers these wise words, 'Create the highest, grandest vision possible for your life because you become what you believe'.

Believing you can succeed and that you deserve your success is at the heart of achieving sustained success. Without that belief, everything becomes incredibly difficult. However, this is only one side of the coin. Many people achieve great success in other people's eyes, but for the achiever, it will never be enough. No matter how many awards, financial rewards, accolades, thanks, and congratulations you may receive, unless you recognise your success, it is an empty achievement. I urge you to use the same criteria to judge your own success as you do to judge others. Celebrate your success, and you will find success comes more easily in the future. With the recognition of your own worth and the fruits of your efforts comes the chance of ongoing happiness and fulfilment.

During your life, you are going to have to make countless choices and deal with many changes. It is important to understand how best to approach these inevitable challenges if you want to sustain a sense of happiness, success, and fulfilment. Secret Pathway 4–Choice provides you with a roadmap of how you can approach decision-making with confidence and deal with the changes and challenges that life and its transitions will inevitably bring.

Chapter 7

Secret Pathway 4–Choice

Secret Pathway Four–Choice focuses on how your choices determine the quality of your life. As you go through life you will experience challenges and significant changes. Physical changes, such as puberty, pregnancy, menopause, illness, disability, and ageing, all bring potential challenges. It is your choice whether you embrace the challenge and see it as an opportunity to grow, or get bogged down and see yourself as a victim with no choice at all.

Changes in circumstances–marriage, divorce, bereavement, moving, a new job, redundancy, or retirement–can be incredibly stressful. Recognising that it is not the challenge that defines you but how you approach and deal with that challenge helps you to navigate the most turbulent times more easily. It is also important to recognise that our greatest personal growth arises out of our facing up to and dealing with life's challenges and transitions.

In the end, everything comes down to recognising that it is absolutely your choice what you believe, whether to love or not and how you deal with things. No one else can decide for you unless you pass the responsibility to them. If you do, then you have to settle for what they choose for you. Please don't think I'm saying it is all plain sailing and easy; I know from personal experience that at times it can feel totally overwhelming. I also know it is our decision whether we stay stuck in the tumult of overwhelm or choose to move forward.

Making the right decisions and managing the changes and transitions in your life can be tricky. This pathway shares a model of motivation, which will help you understand why you make the choices you make and will help you understand what drives and motivates you and the other people in your life. Understanding this gives you the opportunity to choose to do things in the same way or to do things differently, and in doing so, create a different result. The principles and strategies are designed to help you achieve your desired result resourcefully, with ease and grace. The result is greater happiness, success, and fulfilment.

Everything you do is a choice–what you say, how you say it, when you say it, whether you take action, or do nothing. Not making a choice is actually a choice. For many people, it's not choosing to do something and simply letting things drift that has the biggest impact on their lives. Remember, every choice has consequences.

I've had clients who are in a really unhappy relationship or a job they hate, but they stay put. As they stay, their unhappiness grows. They don't confront and deal with any of the problems within the situation, and they don't walk away from the situation either. They choose to stay stuck in what is familiar even though it may be really painful.

In reality, many of these decisions are taken unconsciously. It's important that you make the distinction between doing nothing because you've chosen to do that actively, and doing nothing because you haven't thought things through or you fear to make a decision.

If you always do what you have always done, you will always get what you have now. If you don't like something about your life, it is up to you to change it. If it is a situation which you truly cannot change, you still have the choice to change the way you deal or react to it.

The 7 Underlying Principles and the 7 Connecting Themes

It is no coincidence that I positioned the underlying principles and the connecting themes at the beginning of the book. Each of the principles and themes has a critical role to play in helping you achieve sustained success in every area of your life, but it is in the fabric of every choice you make, minute by minute, day by day that the principles and themes have even greater resonance. Your perspectives, the meaning you make of others' motives, your readiness to forgive, for example, have a profound impact on the choices you make. The way you choose to communicate with yourself and others, whether you do it consciously or it is simply a habitual reflex, will make an enormous difference to the quality of your happiness, success, and whether you feel truly fulfilled or not. It also had the power to influence, belittle, or empower others. It is vital that you take responsibility for every choice you make.

A Victim or Hero? It Is Entirely Your Choice

Throughout your life you will experience a myriad of challenges ranging from the tiny day-to-day ones, like losing your keys, opening the fridge to find the milk has gone sour when you are desperate for a cuppa, being forced to make a detour on your journey to work because a road has been closed. It could also be dealing with someone who is not responding in the manner as you would wish, to big life-changing challenges, such as illness, disability, redundancy, financial ruin, or bereavement.

As I've already pointed out–it is not the challenges that define you, but how you deal with them. You will face many challenges, some out of choice but many will be thrust upon you. Facing a challenging situation can be scary. You may need to engage in a new way of thinking, make incredibly difficult decisions, or cope with a completely different way of life. Please don't think I'm making light of any situation you may find yourself in. The reality is that you have a choice. When life deals you a bum hand, you can choose to be a victim of the set of circumstances you find yourself in or to be a hero or heroine.

Before I go further I need to define what I mean by 'victim' and 'hero' or 'heroine'.

Victims focus on negativity and lack, looking almost exclusively at the things that are going wrong and the things they cannot do. They spend much time wishing things were different. They are likely to believe life isn't fair; they bemoan their lot and stay entrenched in the stage of 'Why me?'.

Victims feel stuck. They will stay in unpleasant even abusive situations rather than deal with the uncertainty that taking action and removing themselves from their current situation would create.

Victims keep themselves small; they fear failure and stay well within their comfort zone. At the same time, they blame their circumstances for why they are stuck in those circumstances. They have no access to their inner resources as their mindsets are firmly focused on the problem. As a result, their brains cannot get into solution mode.

There is a paradox in that victims will often require a great deal of help and support. They are prepared to accept the sort of help which removes the responsibility from them and which does things for them, rather than the help that can give them the tools to help themselves. I have found that those in victim mode are far less likely to accept the sort of help and advice that would allow them to move forward. A big part of the problem is that fear limits a victim's thinking.

I need to make an absolute distinction here. When I talk about 'help and support', I'm not talking about the practical help which allows people to live independently. That is vital, and I know how valuable that is at a personal level. I appreciate hugely the help I've been given over the years, which has enabled me to continue to live independently and carry on working. Even now I get help around the house, driving, and technical and administrative support, all of which empower me.

In contrast to victims, heroes and heroines have a very different mindset. They have a different focus, one based on searching for solutions. They are less inclined to moan about what is going wrong. Debilitating thoughts, like 'Poor me', 'It's all right for you', 'Life isn't fair', are not part of their repertoire. Instead, their thoughts are based on making life even better. They take ownership of their own emotional state and believe the quality of their life is entirely up to them.

Of course, even the greatest hero or heroine will have dark days, times when their situation feels too much and they want things to be different. The difference is, heroes and heroines don't stay in the darkness for long.

They pick themselves up and get on with life. They recognise that the only person who is truly going to create a difference in the quality of their life is themselves. Heroes and heroines own their beliefs, thoughts, and emotional states. They understand that minute by minute it is their choice regarding how they deal with things. They know that even when things are going dreadfully wrong, they have the choice of how they react and deal with the situation. Heroes and heroines look for the gift and the learning, even though these may be difficult to appreciate in the maelstrom of a difficult situation. They think of others as well as themselves, and they choose to get on with their lives in the best way they are able.

Heroes and heroines are not saints. They are just as likely to make mistakes and to feel frustrated and angry at times. The difference is that they move on from that place. They recognise the power of focusing on what they can do and challenge themselves to find a way to move forward. The hero or heroine takes charge of their destiny.

Uncovering Choice in Times of Change and Transition

Change is one of the constants in our lives, yet it creates great levels of anxiety and stress for many people.

When life bumbles along in a routine way, there is little to disrupt our sense of equilibrium. The trouble is, life rarely carries on in that way for long. Understanding what drives and motivates us and others can be enormously helpful. The depth of understanding it creates, expands the choices we have at our disposal when we are faced with change and transition.

It is important to understand that there is nothing good or bad about the way each of us is wired. Each person's unique wiring brings with it benefits and challenges. It is the way we satisfy our needs that makes the difference. It is in this area where there is the greatest capacity to make a difference through our choices. These choices are not only about how we manage ourselves but also about how we work with, react, and engage with others.

Understanding Ourselves and Others

I'm sharing a model of motivation I learned from Tony Robbins. Much of it is based on Abraham Maslow's hierarchy of needs theory that was published in 1943. I've found it useful personally and have taught it to thousands of people through courses and with clients for well over a decade. I have witnessed how understanding this model has changed the way couples relate to one another and how managers and team members have changed the way they manage themselves and others. I hope you will find it interesting and helpful as you become even more aware of the choices you make.

What Drives Us

When you understand yourself and what motivates you, you are well placed to make informed choices. If you are able to understand what motivates others, it is possible to use that to influence them. We are all on the pain-pleasure continuum.

The Pleasure-Pain Continuum

The decision to change any aspect of our lives is governed by the level of pain or pleasure it gives us. Many people settle for what they already have rather than doing what is needed to change things, even though they are not necessarily enjoying life very much. For some people, change becomes an option only when things become so painful that it can no longer be ignored.

Understanding what drives you is helpful; you can then choose to go with your usual pattern of behaviour in any given situation or choose to do things differently. Without this awareness, your choices will be governed by unconscious habitual patterns of thinking and behaviour.

PLEASURE/PAIN CONTINUUM

Avoid Pain ———————— **Seek Pleasure**

People are driven by the need to move toward pleasure or to avoid pain. (The pain may be physical, emotional or spiritual.) Remember one is not better than the other; they are simply different. Those at the outer reach of the continuum will exhibit the features more obviously, but everyone will favour one more than the other.

Driven by Pleasure

People who are driven by achieving pleasure will consistently move towards their goals. They will be clear about what they want and do everything they can to ensure they achieve it. They are likely to be goal setters who know clearly what they want. As soon as one goal is attained they will be onto the next and the next. Each person will have their own definition of what pleasure looks like. Those who are driven by pleasure tend to talk about what they will get, gain, attain, accomplish, have, or obtain. People driven by pleasure will respond better to a carrot than to a stick.

Of course, there is a potential downside, particularly for those on the outer edges of the continuum. When people are always moving towards pleasure, they may not always recognize what they need to avoid. They will often minimize the potential risks and negative consequences of their actions in their desire to achieve their goal.

Pain Avoiders

Other people are motivated by the need to 'move away from', to avoid pain, be it emotional, spiritual, or physical pain. Their decisions are likely to be based on that need. They may take action because they fear what will happen if they don't do something; they fear the consequences. Fear of failing, getting things wrong, being admonished, or being found wanting will potentially outweigh any potential benefits of taking action. People who are driven by pain will talk about what they don't want, the need to move away from, avoid, steer clear of, get rid of, or exclude. People who are driven by avoiding pain often have difficulty in defining and articulating their goals. When asked what they truly want, they may find it easier to say what they don't want.

The downside for people driven by avoiding pain is that the emphasis is on what has, can, or might go wrong, so all these potential problems may lead them to decide not to go forward. There is the potential for people whose major motivator is to avoid pain to sell themselves short. They often work on the principle of 'If I don't try, I can't fail'. They will often resist change unless the language used fits their drive to avoid pain.

Of course, the extent to which people are driven towards achieving pleasure or avoiding pain will differ depending on where they sit on the continuum. Understanding what drives you and how strong that drive is can be really helpful. Self-awareness gives you absolute choice over how you choose to react and behave.

Knowing what drives others offers you the opportunity to adjust the way you approach situations so you serve their needs and achieve your desired outcome.

What Motivates Us

Understanding what motivates you, will enable you to make mindful decisions. Rather than reacting unconsciously, because that is what you have always done, once you identify your motivators, you have the option to decide how and when to react. You also have the choice to do nothing.

Understanding what motivates the people you interact with offers you a really valuable insight into how you can motivate, lead, manage, support, and hold them to account in a constructive way. This is true in both your personal and your professional life.

The 6 Basic Needs

Tony Robbins suggests that we have six basic needs. The first four are the needs of the personality: certainty, uncertainty (variety), significance, and love and connection. Everyone needs all four; however, we all favour two of them. The last two are the needs of the spirit: the need to grow and the need to contribute. These will be extremely important to some people but of little importance to others.

Each of the six needs can be met in a positive, neutral, or negative way. A positive way: they can support good physical, emotional, and spiritual relationships or financial health. A neutral way: they can have no impact on the quality of your life or that of others one way or the other. Negative way: they can be totally destructive, not only to you but also to others in your life.

Six Basic Needs	Potential Vehicles
Certainty	Control, consistency, completion, identity, belief in guidance, faith, food/alcohol/drugs, money
Uncertainty	Lack of control, learned helplessness, stimulating conversation, taking on new challenges, learning, changing focus or tempo, sabotage, new relationships, new locations, new experiences
Significance	Qualifications, possessions, accomplishments, professional success, unique style, making others feel less significant, negative identity, bullying
Love and Connection	Relationships, joining a team/ club/ organisation, being in natural surroundings, self-sacrifice, pets, art, sympathy, gangs, a cause
Growth	The need for physical, emotional, intellectual and spiritual growth
Contribution	Altruism - helping others beyond ourselves, because we genuinely want to

Let's explore each of these six basic needs, so you can develop a better understanding of where both you and the significant people in your life stand in regard to each need.

Need 1: Certainty

The first need is that of certainty. Everyone needs some level of certainty in their life. How much and in what form will vary significantly from person to person. Certainty represents security and survival. Without a sense of certainty that our lives are not in danger, we live in a state of fear. If you were living under a volcano and it was grumbling away, spewing out sulphur and smoke, it is unlikely that you would be able to maintain a sense of certainty and wellbeing.

Maslow identified our most basic needs in this 'certainty' category as air, food, water, warmth, shelter, safety, and sleep. We each have our own list of things which need to be in place in order to make us feel really safe. We have our own definition of security, stability, freedom from fear, and a sense of order.

Our individual needs for certainty have to be satisfied before we feel our survival is assured. There are huge variations in the levels of certainty different people need to feel safe and secure, and as many variations in how each person achieves the certainty, they require. Certainty gives us comfort; we know where we are. There are several potential vehicles for establishing your certainty:

Control

Many people maintain a sense of certainty by controlling their environment: what they eat, being tidy, cleaning, or fixing things. Others will maintain their sense of certainty by controlling other people. It enables them to predict the responses they are likely to get, it makes them feel powerful and in control. It gives them a sense of certainty.

Consistency

Knowing that we have always done things a certain way and that we will continue doing so offers some people the sense of certainty that they crave.

This works in both personal and professional settings. Routines, traditions, rules all serve this purpose.

Completion

People gain certainty by completing things. They will often have endless lists. Ticking them off or crossing them through once the job is completed gives them a needed sense of certainty and satisfaction.

Identity

Certainty can be achieved by having a positive identity, like 'I'm always lucky' or 'I can do it', having a positive attitude, or always helping others. Certainty can also be achieved by having a negative identity, like 'I'm never good enough', 'I'm always unlucky', or 'I always get it wrong'. Either way, people begin to look for evidence to support their beliefs about themselves, good or bad, so a self-fulfilling prophecy becomes perpetuated.

Belief in Guidance

Certainty can come from the belief that your actions are guided by God or some other force, like the Universe, a deity, or a more powerful force..

Faith

Certainty can come from a faith in something bigger than ourselves, either through one of the organized faiths or simply the faith that things will come right in the end. The faith that we are simply enough!

Artificial Vehicles

Some people get their sense of certainty by giving themselves the comfort of food, alcohol, drugs, sex, or shopping. They are certain that it will make them feel better. Even if they know it is doing them harm or that the effect will be short-lived, they crave the comfort and certainty their chosen vehicle offers. It satisfies the need for certainty, even when the person involved knows their chosen vehicle is harming them or their bank balance in the longer term.. It is why so many people struggle to lose weight, to give up smoking, or to stop taking drugs. Trouble is, self-discipline only works in the short term unless the need for certainty is found consistently in another, more productive way. People often require more and more of their chosen 'fix' to get the same 'comfort effect'; if this is the case, it is likely to become an addiction.

Certainty through the Artificial Vehicle of Shopping

To gain an even better understanding of how people use shopping in an attempt to give them a feeling of certainty, let's visit a passage from Rachel Davis's latest International Best Selling novel The Point of Me:

> *Shopping. It truly is an anaesthetic. A modern-day version of laudanum for the middle classes to drift away upon. A potent, economy-driving, legal narcotic. The casual wandering around, the casual reach to run hands along expensive textiles or shiny leather bags or the jewel-like perfume bottles. The casual credit and the casual gratification. Sleepwalking around, looking at things. Things that would confirm one's existence. Possessions that would say something about you to everyone who was looking at you. Say things that you couldn't say for yourself because you were too busy figuring out how the f**k you were going to survive this day. Survive your life. Survive.*

Unsurprisingly, the certainty shopping may give is very short-lived; as soon as the purchase has been made, the sense of satisfaction dissipates. More purchases are required to maintain the shopper's sense of certainty. It is not uncommon for people who use shopping in this way to have lots of unworn clothes still with the labels hanging in their wardrobe or unused purchases cluttering the cupboards. One client who used shopping in this way hid his purchases in the shed; everything was still in its original carrier bag.

Certainty through the Artificial Vehicle of Money

One of the problems with identifying money as a vehicle for certainty is the fear that it will not last, that someone will take it, or that the success which created it will not last. By itself, money is unlikely to create a sense of fulfilment and wellbeing.

Your Relationship with Certainty

Where a person's major driver is certainty, they will work hard to ensure they achieve it on almost any terms. Stability, routine, knowing their place in the order of things is vital. Certainty has to be obtainable and sustainable. Having a sense of control over our lives allows us a feeling of certainty. We can also create that sense of control in a number of negative ways: overeating, anorexia, or other eating disorders, alcohol, working too hard or consistently controlling or blaming others.

Take a moment to consider your relationship with the basic need of certainty. From looking at your habits, choices, and tendencies, how much certainty do you need? What vehicles, both positive and negative, do you use to achieve certainty in your life? By coming to understand how you relate to this need, you allow yourself greater self-awareness and potentially, even more, choices in your life.

The Certainty-Uncertainty Paradox

The paradox is that every one of us needs both certainty and uncertainty. However, we need them in very different ways and to very different degrees. How much uncertainty or change we can manage without feeling stressed determines the quality of our lives.

The way people approach food is a great example of the diversity of approach to certainty and uncertainty. Eating out is an adventure of new flavours, smells, and textures for some people; they love trying new things. Out of choice, they would never eat at the same restaurant twice. For others, anything different is to be avoided. They love to eat the same things all the time as they are certain they will enjoy it.

Life without variety would become boring, stultifying for those who need and enjoy it. Some people are uncertainty junkies. They love the adrenalin rush that they get from jumping out of planes or taking part in extreme sports. Uncertainty can be empowering, such as when we take on a challenging goal or learn a new skill. Travelling to new places or tackling something different can generate tremendous excitement if you are driven by uncertainty. A great deal of growth–intellectual, emotional, and spiritual–can occur during the stimulation caused by uncertainty.

For others, uncertainty represents a challenge, a reason to feel that life is out of control, leading to stress and anxiety. Uncertainty can be incredibly disempowering if it results in your worrying all the time about what might happen, what could go wrong. Anxiety and fear often result in procrastination, in people digging in their heels and being difficult because they feel threatened. It leaves the person feeling un-resourced and stuck.

Take a moment to consider yourself and where you have sought out or shied away from uncertainty.

Is Your Required Balance between Certainty and Uncertainty Set in Stone?

Understanding what makes you feel safe and comfortable is important. You can then check in with the situation: You can ask yourself if the need to feel comfortable and safe is more important than the opportunity offered by the change you face. In that moment, you have the gift of choice. You can stay within your comfort zone or choose to be uncomfortable for a while in order to achieve the outcome created by the change in question.

I've had the privilege of working with many people who are struggling with change and uncertainty. Their situations have varied enormously, including leaving home for the first time, changing jobs, facing redundancy, getting a promotion, marrying or divorcing, moving home, dealing with menopause, dealing with an empty nest, retiring, and facing illness, disability, and bereavement. The one thing they all have in common is that everyone initially struggled with the changes life presented them, but then they each found a new equilibrium and a greater sense of strength as they learned to deal with the challenge. The same will be true for you.

Excellence

Aristotle said, 'We are what we repeatedly do. Excellence, then, is not an act, but a habit'.

In a recent article Richard Branson explored the relationship he has with his need for adventure, surprise, and challenge and his recognition that the certainty created through on-going repetition can ensure excellence. He outlines how he has developed habits (routines), which underpin his health and his business success. For example, he has an early morning routine which includes exercise, meditation, and drinking lots of water. Once completed he is set up for the day.

It is up to each of us to create our own balance between our need for certainty and uncertainty and to choose the vehicles to achieve both in as positive a way as possible. It is entirely your choice how you deal with your life, moment by moment. If you are finding things difficult, choose to get help and support.

Need 2: Uncertainty or Variety

Life would be boring without uncertainty or variety. Humans are naturally curious. Our need to understand the world and how it works, and to discover new places and different ways of doing things have shaped the modern world. Without this thirst for something new, this longing for uncertainty and variety, we would still be living in caves.

The human race may collectively have the desire to expand its horizons and to challenge the status quo, but at an individual level there is an enormous difference in the ways we achieve our need for certainty (security, safety, routine, structure, familiarity) and our need for uncertainty (variety, change, challenge, adventure, something new and different). We all need some variety, excitement, surprises, and a sense of challenge. Uncertainty provides just that.

As with all six basic needs, there are times when satisfying our need for uncertainty results in negative behaviours. Here are a few examples:

The need for uncertainty can create the drive to change jobs constantly. The result is the person involved never has to take the responsibility for seeing things through. Because of this, they are unlikely to reach their potential. The need for uncertainty can result in a series of broken relationships. As soon as a relationship looks as if it is becoming too certain and significant, a person will end it. This behaviour is driven by a fear of what certainty might demand: commitment. The need for uncertainty may be so strong such that it can dominate and overcome a person's values of trust and fidelity. When a relationship becomes boring, such a person will start an affair to create a sense of danger and uncertainty. The need for uncertainty can drive some people to pick a row when things become too certain. They enjoy the thrill of the parry and thrust of the argument. This can be incredibly challenging for other people.

Need 3: Significance

The third need, significance, comes in many forms: a sense of being needed, a feeling of importance, a sense of purpose, or a sense of meaning or uniqueness.

As with the other needs, our need for significance can have a positive, neutral, or negative impact on our lives and the lives of those around us. We all need to feel validated, to have some sense that we matter to others. Feeling that we are seen and heard and that we have some significance to others is important, particularly when people lack confidence or a robust sense of self-worth. Many of the people I have worked with over the years have struggled with feeling that they don't matter, that they have no voice or feeling rejected and worthless.

The need to feel significant drives our behaviours in many ways. It can spur on athletes, scholars, musicians, entrepreneurs, and others to work incredibly hard to achieve and sustain excellence. It can also have less positive outcomes: It can lead children to behave more and more badly to get the attention they crave, or adults to indulge in inappropriate behaviours that make them stand out. Those who always put others first, those who are constantly helpless or always have something wrong with them often do it so that they are noticed - these behaviours are driven by the need to achieve some level of significance. In reality, everyone wants to feel seen, heard, and valued. People involved are usually completely unaware of their underlying needs and how that impacts on their behaviours. It is simply how they are.

It is common for significance to be one of the preferred needs of highly successful business leaders. They need to succeed and to be seen to be doing well. You may well hear them say things like 'There is no room for failure', 'I always strive for excellence', or 'I'm ambitious and want to be the best at what I do'.

Some people get their sense of significance and self-worth by doing things for others. They put their own needs below that of everyone else, often at a cost to their health and wellbeing.

Those who use violence always have significance as a major driver; certainty will be their other preferred motivator. Someone holding a gun to your head or beating you has a very particular sort of significance. Those who play power games need to feel significant and in control.

Houses, jewellery, tattoos, cars, holidays, voluntary work, and hobbies offer people a sense of significance. Some get their significance from the clothes they wear. They may wear only designer clothes, they may boast that all their clothes come from charity or thrift shops, or they may insist that all their clothes are handmade. The outward manifestation may be different, but the motivation is to feel significant.

How do you achieve your need for significance? Is the vehicle you have chosen to make you feel valued and significant a positive one? How important is significance to you?

Understanding what motivates you and why and how you achieve that sense of motivation is really important. It is only when you understand yourself, and only then, that you can make an active choice to consciously choose to continue in the same way or if necessary, to gain that sense of significance in a more positive way.

Need 4: Love and Connection

Humans are dependent on others for many years. At the start of our lives, our very survival is dependent on another human being putting our needs before their own. Mothers are chemically conditioned to love their children at birth when there is a surge of oxytocin to mothers' brains. Initially, most babies experience complete and unconditional love. They see themselves at the heart of the universe; their needs are paramount.

The behaviours which many people demonstrate throughout their lives are based on the lessons learnt very early in life. We create beliefs about ourselves based on that experience. We continue to interpret our lives through those early experiences. Over time they become unconscious habits which are rarely challenged.

As very young children we are conditioned to behave in certain ways to achieve attention and love. Some learn that to get noticed they have to be the perfect student; others will only get attention when they are ill or very helpful. As we grow up, it is inevitable that we experience situations where we are ignored, chastised, or hurt. We often carry the result of how that early experience made us feel into adulthood. When people don't get the love and attention they need, they will look for consolation in other ways, such as eating, drinking alcohol, taking drugs, working excessive hours, being promiscuous, or pleasing others to the exclusion of serving their own needs.

Our need for love and connection is met through bonding, a sense of oneness, sharing, intimacy, feeling a part of, being at one with, all of which give us a sense of meaning.

The Significance-Love and Connection Paradox

Whilst we all need both significance and love and connection in our lives, we will favour one of these two needs. There is a paradox between the need for significance and for love and connection. Many people settle for significance when what they really want is love because significance feels safer; there is far less chance of feeling vulnerable and exposed. In the same way, many people will settle for connections with friends, family, colleagues, their neighbours, or their pets when what they really desire is romantic love.

Do you favour love and connection over significance? Do you crave true love but settle for connection or significance because they feel safer because you don't have to let others see your vulnerability?

Unless you know whether love is a major motivator and you appreciate whether fear is holding you back, it would be all too easy to settle for the safer option. Once you understand what really motivates you, it is then possible to make any changes necessary to help you achieve your ideal outcome successfully.

Needs 5 & 6: Spiritual Needs of Growth and Contribution

For some, the spiritual needs, which are to grow and to contribute, are incredibly important. Their lives are enhanced by embracing these needs; they are major motivators in their lives. For others, the spiritual needs have no appeal or importance.

To Grow

The fifth need, the need to develop and grow physically, emotionally, intellectually, or spiritually, is extremely strong in some people.

My dad was constantly learning. He was a teacher most of his life, and even in his late eighties, he was still studying with the WEA (Workers'

Education Association). One of the prerequisites for the classes to keep running was that a certain number of assignments were to be submitted each term to the university. His class was full of retired people who loved the classes but were far less enthusiastic about doing the assignments. Dad loved doing the research and delving into whatever subject he was studying, so he did everyone's assignments, thereby ensuring the classes continued. My dad, then, is a solid example of someone with a high need for intellectual growth.

To Contribute

Contributing is the sixth need. Contributing to something beyond ourselves because we want to, rather than because we think we ought to, gives some people great satisfaction. It is my belief that contribution has the capacity to provide us with the greatest sense of fulfilment and purpose.

Success without fulfilment often feels empty. Many people appear to have it all, all the trappings of success: a well-paid, remarkable career, money, a big house, a fast car. a wife and family they love, yet they feel unfulfilled. Look at how many well-known, high-profile people have found true fulfilment and purpose from helping others, like Bill and Melinda Gates. The same is true for us all. Caring about others and making a positive difference in whatever way we can, has the capacity to bring us all fulfilment.

One way to practice the need to contribute is by doing random acts of kindness on a daily basis. They don't have to cost you money, just a bit of thought. Letting someone out in heavy traffic, opening the door, offering to help someone with their bag, and paying for someone's coffee are small acts of kindness, which can brighten the day of a stranger and at the same time serve your need to contribute. Don't look for any acknowledgement or thanks because random acts of kindness are not about significance; they are about contribution.

Think about what is important to you. What makes you excited to get up in the morning or picks you up when you are feeling low?

Is your physical, intellectual, emotional, and spiritual growth an important and ongoing part of your life? Does learning something new make you feel good? Understanding what makes you feel energised and fully alive is an essential factor in whether you feel truly fulfilled.

How does helping others and making a contribution make you feel? Is it an integral part of your life, or are you happy to leave it to others?

This model of motivation is an expansion of Maslow's hierarchy of needs. It offers those who choose to use it, a way of understanding their own motivation and that of others. Why is that important? When you have an awareness of what really motivates you and the reason for it, it becomes possible to make a deliberate choice to satisfy that need in the most positive and effective way. Understanding what motivates others, gives you an enormous advantage whether you are dealing with your partner, children, family, friends, work colleagues, team, or boss. It is true gold!

Addiction and the 6 Needs

Every activity we undertake gives us some form of feedback. That feedback can make us feel good (positive), have little impact (neutral), or make us feel awful (negative). Tony Robbins believes that any activity that gives us satisfaction at a 7 or more out of 10 in three or more of the six basic needs is likely to become an addiction.

Let me give you a personal example. I am a recovering workaholic. Let's look at why work became somewhat of an addiction for me whilst I was a headteacher (principal). I loved the job; it gave me a great sense of certainty. I was in a position of authority, so I had control over many of the decisions that were made. I could choose when to delegate, when to involve others, and when to take things on myself. There were many daily, weekly, and termly routines; the school had many traditions, some of which I introduced.

There was enormous variety within the role. No two days were the same. I dealt with a myriad of different situations, one moment dealing with a naughty child, another training staff, yet another discussing drains or building repairs with the site manager or a contractor. I had to create new curriculum, develop new training programmes, do the budget, chair meetings, and keep up with the plethora of governmental directives. I was never bored!

My need for significance was completely satisfied. I was well-respected by the pupils, staff, parents, and the local authority. I was often asked by the powers that be to help run training sessions at the National College of School Leadership and the London Institute. I was invited to be an advisor by the DFES, a government department in charge of education. The school achieved many accolades, awards, and kite marks during my leadership, and we were on the 'Best 100 Schools' list twice during my tenure as the head.

Being the head of the school gave me enormous opportunities for love and connection. Many of the staff have become life-long personal friends. I have several Godchildren as a result. I had very positive relationships with my pupils and their parents. Even today it gives me great pleasure when I meet past pupils, their parents, and grandparents, which happens quite often, even though I have now moved seventy miles away. I love to hear how they are doing.

The job involved endless opportunities to grow and learn, and contribution lay at the heart of everything I did. Growing, learning, and contributing gave me a huge sense of enjoyment, satisfaction and fulfilment.

An extra bonus was that being so involved in the job provided me with great pain control. Whilst I was engaged in doing something I loved and was of such value, my focus was on that, rather than how my body was complaining.

Whilst I was working as a head, each of my motivational needs was consistently satisfied at a 9 or 10 out of 10, so it is little wonder I became a workaholic.

Work satisfied so many of my needs. Not only did it give me immense satisfaction because I was making a really positive difference doing something I loved, but it also satisfied my need for security and structure. I had bags of variety, status, and significance, and I had the close connection created via staff, parents, and pupils. Most of my long-term friends have come through my work as a head. I was constantly learning and making what I believed to be a considerable contribution.

What is perhaps less obvious are the downsides to my work addiction, namely how being so absorbed in my work blinded me–or helped me to blind myself–to other very significant aspects of myself. Let me explain: When I am interested and involved in what I do, I become less aware of my physical pain, which is one of the constants in my life since the ski accident. I focus on the external things I have influence over, and in doing so, my body becomes far less insistent. This has been a double-edged sword. Whilst it has been incredibly useful on a day-to-day basis, I think part of the reason for the deterioration of my health is that at times I pushed my body far harder than was wise.

One of the things I have found difficult to recognise until recent years is that I used my work as an emotional anaesthetic. It helped me manage the pain of losing the lifestyle I thought I would have had prior to the accident. Grieving for what might have been, is something which can feel deeply challenging and needs to be dealt with, or it has a habit of popping up at the most inconvenient times. Looking back, much of my grieving took place after I left headship in 2004.

Being a workaholic offered lots of positives–pain control, purpose, a sense of achievement, a community, and great satisfaction–but there were also casualties.

For me, the biggest of those casualties was that I never made any time to create a close, loving personal relationship with one special person. Work became a safe excuse not to put me into a place of huge vulnerability. Term time would be so frantic there was no time to consider my personal life. The summer holidays were the only time when I could breathe and allow myself any significant 'me-time'.

My tentative attempts to find someone special were clothed in disaster (that's for another book). The men I met were either so wrapped up in their own issues that I found myself giving free coaching, or they couldn't see past the wheelchair and see me for who I was. It was such a relief when the autumn term time started again, and I could retreat to a place where I felt valued, happy, and secure.

Like most people who have had an addiction, it is all too easy to slip back into old ways of being, so I have to be mindful that whilst my work is incredibly important to me, it is not all of who I am. I am now far more comfortable with being vulnerable, but it is still a work in progress. I know that I will find that special someone, and I'm taking active steps to help it along.

I'm sharing this with you for a few reasons. Firstly, to exemplify how such an addiction to some of these 6 basic needs can play out in all of its positives and negatives. I hope that by being so open about my work addiction you'll take the cue and find the courage–as I assure you I had to do!–to lovingly yet totally consider yourself and the upsides and downsides to a seemingly benign addiction that you might have too. Second, I want you to know that I too I'm a 'work in progress' – I work providing guidance and counsel to others on their journey to living as their best, most genuine self, and I too am on the same journey. We are in this together! And the fact that I am making progress on this journey as well as continuing to work at my greater and greater personal goals and dreams, I think has put me in a fabulous position to provide real, hands-on support to so many others. And as I see it, we're in this together, or we should be! That's why I can't encourage you enough to join the Thrive Together Tribe!

Recognising Others' Primary Needs to Shape Your Best Future

There is a huge difference between what we learn to live with and the potential quality of life we could achieve when we are not prepared to settle for second best.

In each situation in your daily life, you need to be clear about the outcome you are trying to achieve and why. Each situation will require a different approach. It is the ability to be flexible, to understand your own needs, and to be able to read the needs of others and engage them in the process that will determine the extent to which you will influence and motivate others. Once you understand yourself and what motivates you and how you achieve it, you have an absolute choice whether to satisfy it in the way you have always done or to choose a more constructive vehicle if required.

Once you understand what motivates others (their strongest needs) and how they achieve them, you have the opportunity to motivate them more effectively by changing the language you use and the way in which you interact with them. When you recognise that certainty is a major motivator for one of your team, clients, or bosses, you can approach things accordingly. If you know and understand what already motivates and influences the other person and why it is so, then you can begin to appreciate the world from their perspective. Motivation and influence of others become much easier.

The Role of Choice in Life's Transitions

From Child to Adult

As children, we rely on parents, carers, and teachers to set the parameters of what we can and cannot do. Children quickly learn to push the boundaries and to challenge the things they do not like. Parents, carers, and teachers facilitate children's understanding of choice and consequence. For some, this is very clearly defined, and for others much less so. Generally speaking, children want to please, and this colours many of the choices they make.

By the time children reach their teens, their peer group has a much greater influence on the choices they make. The need to fit in and belong is incredibly strong. This leads to a certain set of choices, some of which will be very different to those parents would approve of.

By the time we reach adulthood, it is presumed that we are in total charge of the choices we make. In my experience, this is not the case for many people. Their choices are bound by pleasing others or wanting to fit in. Some are so busy ensuring they do what others want and expect of them that they fail to identify what they really want themselves. When they do identify what they want, some people choose not to do it to avoid upsetting anyone.

Our emotional age has nothing to do with the number of birthdays we have celebrated. I've known children who show incredible maturity, providing stability and common sense for their friends and even, in some circumstances, for their parents. I've met adults who may have lived for several decades but are trapped in a much younger emotional body. They have a tantrum when things don't go their way; they sulk if crossed and are still stuck in believing their needs are the only ones that matter.

Being the emotional grown up, means taking total responsibility for your actions and choices, for the quality of your life and for your own happiness.

The Happiness Challenge–Why Not Choose to Try It?

Most people set out a huge list of criteria which need to be satisfied before they will be happy: a great job, a big house, a new car, lots of holidays, a fantastic body, a soulmate who loves them unconditionally and never argues, children who tidy their bedroom and do their homework without arguing, and, and, and ......

As a result, happiness remains elusive. The same people will often feel very easily rejected or hurt. Their list of criteria for feeling negative emotions is, by contrast, very short; they trigger negative emotions far more easily.

It is your choice whether you make it easy or difficult to feel good or not. Changing the balance requires a new habit to be installed. The Happiness Challenge is designed to help you install the habit of starting the day with a smile and the intention of feeling happy during the day. I challenge you to choose to be happy; I challenge you to try out the Happiness Challenge.

Choosing to Be Happy

As you wake up in the morning, before you get out of bed do the 'Funky Chicken' Happiness Challenge:

- Put your hands on your waist, elbows out.
- Waggle your elbows as if they were a pair of chicken wings.
- If you can't feel the sides of your coffin, it means you are alive.
- Say to yourself, 'It is a new day. I choose to be happy!'

Of course, it feels a bit ridiculous–but that's the point. It is silly, so you smile, and if you smile at the beginning of the day, it starts you off in a positive way. The body secretes the feel-good hormones: endorphins, serotonin, and dopamine.

A smile is a good way to start your day, so why not give it a try? Remember that installing a new habit takes 28 days of doing the same thing consistently to create a new neural pathway. If you want any behaviour to become a powerful new habit, you will have to start from the beginning again if you give up halfway through.

It also makes sense to ensure that the habits you are establishing are empowering and support your physical, mental, and spiritual well-being, rather than those habitual ways of thinking, speaking, or acting that keep you stuck, unhealthy, poorly resourced, and feeling small.

If You Want Things to Change, You Have to Do Something Different.

Today is the beginning of the rest of your life. It is entirely up to you to let things continue exactly as they are, or if you want things to change, to do something different.

Einstein's definition of madness is to keep doing the same things and expect different results. Amazingly we do it, all the time. In fact, when things go wrong, we do the same thing over and over again simply hoping that by chance they'll result in things going the 'right' way–though that is highly unlikely to happen. We think by doing it harder, more frequently, louder, or longer, that things will be different this time.

If you are behaving in a way which is not serving you, it's time to do something differently. You can choose to continue banging your head against a brick wall and give yourself a headache, or you can choose to do something new and achieve a different result. The choice is yours.

It Is Not the Grand Gesture That Makes the Difference.

Remember, it is not the grand gesture that makes the difference. It is small actions consistently taken over time that create sustained change. Not sustaining the line of action or following up is one of the most common causes of failure.

How many people do you know who've wanted to lose weight after Christmas? They go on a diet and are determined to stick to a low-calorie regime. For the first few days, they exist on salad. They go to the office on Thursday, and it is someone's birthday. There is a large chocolate cake on offer. They break their diet and then feel bad about having done so. Because they feel bad about their actions, they start to beat themselves up. By the time they get home, they are feeling terrible, so they attack the biscuit tin. They then think there is no point in carrying on with their diet that day and decide to start their diet again the following Monday. On the intervening days, they alternately criticise themselves for their weakness and comfort themselves with food because they feel so awful. In the end, they put on more weight.

What makes the difference are the small changes that are consistently done over time. If you're going to make a change and you want that to become a new habit, you have to create a new neural pathway. You now know it takes 28 days of doing the same thing every day over and over again to create a new neural pathway. As the new behaviour becomes established, it becomes a part of what you do and eventually who you are.

Your choices, even the seemingly little ones, have such an incredible impact on the quality of your life and that of those connected with you. It is far too important to allow your decisions to be made at an unconscious, habitual level. Every choice you make contributes to your happiness, how successful you are, and whether you are living your life's purpose. These, in turn, contribute to your level of fulfilment, so it makes absolute sense to make these choices mindfully.

We have now explored the 7 Underpinning Principles, the 7 Connecting Themes and the first four of the five Secret Pathways. Each has much to offer individually; implementing the ideas and strategies of any one of the chapters has the capacity to make a positive difference to your life. And collectively–wow–they combine to provide you with the tools and information you need to navigate the challenges of life's journey with tremendous joy and satisfaction and much-reduced levels of stress. Everything we have covered so far has been in preparation for the final secret pathway–that of purpose and fulfilment.

Chapter 8

Secret Pathway 5–Purpose and Fulfilment

Secret Pathway 5 provides you with the opportunity to examine your spiritual journey. Many people reach a point in their lives where they have achieved much, but still, have that aching thought, 'Is this it?' Understanding our personal purpose in life is a vital element to achieving a sense of true fulfilment. Here, we shall explore how to access your intuition in order to give yourself permission to follow your dreams and live your passion, and in doing so achieve consistent happiness and the joy of true fulfilment.

Fulfilment comes from living a life of purpose, but this is different for every individual. True fulfilment comes from seeing yourself as a spiritual being, at one with the Creator, Universal Energy, God. It emanates from the sense of belonging, of seeing the similarities rather than the differences between yourself and others, of knowing that, the way in which you care for yourself, others, and the Earth itself, really matters.

Do you feel fulfilled? Do you have a sense of purpose? How satisfied are you with your life? Does it feel complete? Do you find yourself feeling as if there is something you can't quite define that is missing? This is not about success–lots of people achieve significant success professionally and personally but still feel as if there is something else required to make their lives feel complete. I suggest the missing link is a sense of purpose and fulfilment.

Finding Your Purpose

Your purpose and the happiness and fulfilment that come with finding it are closer than you think. They may feel elusive, but they are there and have always been there. Finding your purpose requires you to be aware enough to recognise it. This becomes so much easier when you stop trying too hard when you give yourself the space to 'be'.

Our life's purpose is more about living a life of appreciation, gratitude, the meaning you make of your life, and the contribution you make. The meaning becomes clearer when you use your considerable strengths and talents in the service of others and in the process of self-discovery. Being open to new experiences and new ways of thinking, stepping out of your comfort zone, and being ready and willing to fail and learn from that failure will not only help you define your true purpose but will also help motivate and inspire others to do the same.

The Keys to Achieving Happiness and Fulfilment

Those who have a great sense of purpose and fulfilment have certain things in common:

- They recognise that they are enough.
- They recognise that purpose and fulfilment are not to be found in material things.
- They understand that time spent serving the needs of others creates a huge sense of purpose and fulfilment.
- They understand the importance of playing full-out.
- They appreciate the power of laughter, playfulness, and light in their lives.
- They take full responsibility for bringing joy into their lives and the lives of others rather than expecting others to manufacture it for them.
- They live every day in a way that ensures there is no need for regret.
- They recognise that life isn't always easy or uncomplicated. They make the best of each situation, recognising that greater learning takes place in times of turbulence and challenge. They believe

everything we learn is preparing us for something greater. They make lemonade out of the lemons life brings.

- They challenge themselves to ever greater heights.
- They appreciate the natural world and do what they can to preserve it.
- They are appreciative and grateful and share with others.
- They have faith in themselves and in the goodness of life and what it offers.

You Are Enough!

It is only when you believe that you are enough just as you are, that you can feel truly fulfilled. The first and most important lesson for us all to believe is we are enough just as we are. Learning to love and appreciate yourself just as you are, for all your gifts and your imperfections, is vital if you are to achieve lasting happiness and fulfilment.

Interestingly, the feeling of not being enough, of being inadequate, can initially spur people on to achieve even greater things. However, in that lies a challenge: No matter how impressive your successes may be to the world at large, it will never be enough to make you feel great, unless you recognise your own worth.

Those who are motivated to strive for ever greater and greater levels of achievement simply in order to feel better about themselves put their health and wellbeing at risk. Feelings of satisfaction and achievement, however well-deserved, are at best short-lived, and the feelings of needing to achieve more, tend to increase rather than diminish over time. This route leads to burnout, frustration, or depression. This has been one of my greatest life lessons.

The feeling of not measuring up leads some people to a cycle of addiction as they attempt to anaesthetize themselves from the painfully negative emotions generated as a result. Addictions involving food, alcohol, drugs, sex, hoarding, and shopping are all commonly underpinned by a sense of being unworthy, unlovable, or inadequate.

Self-worth, confidence, acceptance, and the belief that you deserve success are lovable and have the capacity to love; all emanate from the core belief that you are enough, complete just as you are. This is nothing about ego; it is trusting the inner wisdom that you are enough as you are–an infinite being, connected to source. To be happy, successful, and fulfilled requires an acceptance that you are not broken; it requires a solid self-belief.

I heard Marisa Peer, a well-known hypnotherapist who works with the rich and famous, speak some time ago. She described how she was phoned by the producer of a television company who wanted her to work with one of the actors who was being a bit of a 'prima donna'. He was threatening to leave the show halfway through a long TV series. Marisa agreed.

Then the producer asked her, 'What car do you drive?'

She was a bit taken aback and said, 'I drive a Mustang'.

The producer replied, 'That's no good. You'll have to hire a Ferrari or a Maserati; otherwise, he won't have the car on his drive'.

When the actor opened the door to her, he was not pleased when he saw her car. She had driven her Mustang.

He did eventually invite Marisa in, complaining, 'I don't know why you're here, you can't help me'.

She replied, 'Just give me ten minutes. I think I've got a pretty good idea of what your problem is already'.

She asked him about his childhood. He told her his father had been a very strict man and that he hadn't approved of his becoming an actor. When the actor had gone against his father's wishes, his father had cast him off and disinherited him. They hadn't spoken since. His father died before he'd become famous.

Having listened to the actor, Marisa suggested to him that his problem was he believed he wasn't enough. No amount of wealth, possessions, or fame would ever make him happy unless he believed in himself.

Marisa set him the following activity. She wrote, 'I AM ENOUGH!' on every mirror in his house with red lipstick. She also had him write, 'I AM

ENOUGH!' as a screensaver on his computer and on his phone. She asked him to say the words out loud every time he encountered the message. She told him how important it was that he say the words aloud with real conviction several times a day.

A few weeks later she got a phone call from him admitting, 'I now know what you're getting at. I realize I don't need all the material trappings to make me feel better. I feel happy.'

A few months later he phoned to share, 'I'm doing really well. I've got a great new girlfriend, not a model like I always used to date, but somebody who's a real person and somebody who I think I can love'.

I was really impressed with the results and wanted to test the process out for myself. I decided to try the exercise myself and at the same time with a group of women who attended the personal development group I was working with. I created I AM ENOUGH posters for them rather than using lipstick (it's the very devil to clean off mirrors). I was interested to see what impact it would have on them and on me. I asked them to put the posters in places where they would see them frequently during the day: on mirrors, the back of the bathroom door, the wardrobe, the fridge, etc. I asked them to put it as a screensaver on their computers and on their phones. They were asked to say the words aloud in a particular way, to repeat the words with the emphasis on a different word each time. I impressed upon them the need to say the words with real conviction.

I AM ENOUGH

I **AM** ENOUGH

I AM **ENOUGH**

After practising it for a month, I was amazed at its positive effect on me and was curious how the other women had got on. At the next meeting, four weeks later, they all talked about how transformational this single exercise had been. They felt better about themselves; they reported feeling far more confident and assertive. What was even more impressive was that they maintained the increased sense of self-worth over time.

I've since used it with hundreds of people, and the results have been amazing! So, I'm urging you to try 'I am enough', because it's true: YOU ARE ENOUGH!

I have created sets of beautiful posters all ready to post around the house. There are 2 sets of flowers and two sets of scenes in nature. You can find these on my website. https://genuinely-you.com

Get your children to do the I am enough exercise too. Give them the gift of recognising they are enough early in life. Developing a positive sense of self-worth will help them develop confidence, resilience, and the ability to withstand the challenges life will inevitably bring. Their journey to happiness, success, and fulfilment will be all the easier as a result.

Material Wealth

Many people spend their lives accruing material wealth and possessions or aspiring to greater material wealth. Easy credit has made the acquiring of material things so much easier and more prevalent. If you visit a shopping mall on a Saturday, you will see many people buying 'stuff' they don't need and, in all probability, won't wear or use more than a few times. Many are trying to fill a void. The excitement of the purchase gives the illusion of happiness, but it is very short-lived, so off they go again and again and again. The Internet makes it even easier to feed this habit 24/7.

Big houses, fast cars, expensive jewellery, and any amount of purchases will not make you feel truly happy and fulfilled in the long term. Of course, financial abundance is wonderful, as it offers financial security, comfort, and choice, but it doesn't bring a sense of true fulfilment and purpose. It is also possible to have a great sense of happiness and fulfilment without all the trappings of financial success. This comes from having a sense of true purpose.

Abundance

I believe abundance is about so much more than money. Love, laughter, connection, learning, new experiences, comfort, sharing, giving, receiving–

everyone's list will be different. Of course, money is an important element, but it is what you do with it which makes the difference, as Ebenezer Scrooge discovered in 'A Christmas Carol'.

Over the centuries, many extremely wealthy people have realised that their great wealth did not mean a life of happiness, fulfilment, and purpose until they started to use their significant wealth for the good of others. Modern-day philanthropists, like Bill Gates and Warren Buffett, have discovered that all their incredible wealth has taken on a far more satisfying meaning, once they decided to use it as a means to do good. It is in creating opportunities for others where they have found a satisfying sense of purpose and fulfilment.

Are You Happy?

Being fulfilled and happy is very much your choice. Ultimately if you don't like the way your life is going, you have the opportunity to either change your life or to change the way you feel about it.

I didn't like being in a wheelchair, but that was my reality. I could choose to spend my life bemoaning the fact, or I could choose to look for the gift. Of course, it was a challenge to choose to see the gift of my situation, but doing so meant I have had a far better quality of life.

Ultimately when you look for the gift in any difficult situation, you'll find it, but you have to look. The gift for me was finding a unique way of developing leadership, both within myself and my school. In doing so, I developed strategies, which proved to be very successful at both a personal and organisational level. The same strategies have proved to be very successful for the countless individuals and wide range of organisations I've worked with since. There's always something positive to take from every day, even on those days that feel dark and challenging.

Each phase of life brings its own rhythm, its high points and its challenges. It is through these experiences that we develop an understanding of what is important to us. All of those experiences, good, bad, and indifferent, help us determine what is really important in life, what provides us with a sense of purpose and fulfilment. Learning what gives each of us a sense of purpose and fulfilment is a very individual process. Some have the great fortune to know what makes them feel whole from a very early age. If they follow their instincts and stay true to their purpose, they will find themselves living a truly happy and fulfilling life.

Those who have a great sense of purpose but disregard it for some reason, will struggle to feel fulfilled and at peace with themselves. The reasons behind ignoring that 'knowing' are many and various. A lack of belief in themselves, parental or other people's expectations, or being put off by a lack of resources or opportunity can all knock people off course. Life becomes more stressful, and there is a potentially negative impact on health and wellbeing.

I have also worked with a number of people who have not yet recognised what their purpose in life may be. Without a sense of purpose, their life lacks direction and definition. They feel as if they were going through the motions but find life unfulfilling. Those who have finally identified their purpose and passion, and made the decision to follow where that path took them, have experienced an incredible difference to the quality of their lives. They've found the rewards amazing.

Purpose is not necessarily about your job or work. One client gets a huge sense of fulfilment from rescuing cats, another from painting, yet another from her spiritual practice. However, if you can earn your living doing something you are passionate about, something which fulfils your true purpose, it is a great blessing.

The 7 Underlying Principles, the 7 Connecting Themes and the first 4 Secret Pathways are there to help you on your journey to happiness and fulfilment. It is up to you to determine what changes will enhance the quality of your life and that of those around you, challenging those beliefs which no longer serve you, or developing a more positive relationship with yourself. You may find the thought of implementing change daunting, but it will be well worth the investment of time and energy as the reward is that inner glow of fulfilment and joy, which will sustain you for the rest of your life.

Just like you, I continue to develop and grow emotionally and spiritually as I experience life. One of the major motivations for creating the Thrive Together Tribe is to provide a safe space where we can explore and share the experiences of our spiritual journeys, find solutions to the blocks, define, and celebrate what has contributed to our sense of purpose, and celebrate those things which have generated lasting happiness, joy, and fulfilment.

Ego vs. Inner Wisdom

Learning to distinguish between the thoughts and ideas that are led by our ego versus our inner wisdom or God Spark is eloquently described by the late Wayne Dyer, an American philosopher, self-help author, and motivational speaker. In his book Being and Balance from 2016, he wrote the following:

> *The ego-idea of yourself is very much like the mirror example, without the adjustments. Your ego wants you to look for the inside on the outside. The outer illusion is the major preoccupation of the ego.*
>
> *The ego-idea has been with us ever since we began to think. It sends us false messages about our true nature. It leads us to make assumptions about what will make us happy and we end up frustrated. It pushes us to promote our self-importance while we yearn for a deeper and richer life experience. It causes us to fall into the void of self-absorption, again and again, not knowing that we need only shed the false idea of who we are.*
>
> *Our true self is eternal. It is the God force within us. The way of our higher self is to reflect our inner reality rather than the outer illusion. The description given by Sogyal Rinpoche in The Tibetan Book of Living and Dying is a wonderful explanation of this discovery: "Two people have been living in you all of your life. One is the ego, garrulous, demanding, hysterical, calculating; the other is the hidden spiritual being, whose still voice of wisdom you have only rarely heard or attended to." He refers to this hidden spiritual being as our wise guide.*

When we learn to transcend the illusions sponsored by the ego, we can access this wise guide. We can invite in the higher aspects of ourselves to function in their natural, loving, and integrated design.

Learning to Listen to Your Wise Guide

When you allow yourself the time and space to access your inner wisdom-your wise guide, offers you a great route to developing a sense of what is truly important. It facilitates the journey to understanding and embracing your purpose and the achievement of fulfilment.

In the busy, noisy, technology-filled lives we all live, you have to make a deliberate decision to stop, even for a few moments. Think about where you get your best ideas. When are you most in tune with yourself and nature? What sparks your creativity.

Whether you choose meditation, sitting quietly in the sunshine, staring into a winter fire, gardening, running, singing, or being in the shower for a few extra minutes, choose to let go of the noise and distractions, and tune into your inner wisdom. Ask the question, 'What does the wise one say?'

Slowing Things Down–Becoming a Human Being Rather Than a Human Doing

Most of us are rushing around chasing our tails, trying to reduce our to-do list to manageable proportions. We have become human doings rather than human beings. In the struggle to satisfy all the expectations heaped upon us, including the even more demanding ones we set ourselves, it is all too easy to lose the sense of who we are and what is really important.

It is impossible to make contact with the inner you, your intuition, your wise guide, unless you find time to simply be. It is in stillness and silence that you can access the power and capacity to cut through the white noise and interference. Giving yourself the time to quieten your busy mind, contemplate, and breathe, opens the door to infinite possibilities.

It is something I'm learning to do, but it has not been without its challenges. Being in a quiet, meditative state is in direct contradiction to my upbringing. On those rare occasions when my parents found me doing nothing; I was told to go and find something useful to do. It is only now that I recognise the enormous power of those still moments when you allow yourself to connect with the inner you, where it becomes so much easier to access the full power of your intuition.

'Being' requires you to be in the moment. To fully experience everything that moment offers requires you to get out of your own way, let go of the worries, the endless conversations in your head about what you should, shouldn't, ought, or need to be doing, and to be fully present.

Once each moment has passed, there is no getting it back. Without the capacity to focus on the present moment, much of your life will be based on looking back on things you have no power to change, or looking forward, worrying about things which might never happen.

Even the most urbane activities offer you the choice to approach them in different ways: Do them mindlessly, seeing them as simply jobs to tick off the list; or consider them as opportunities to savour the moment, to explore your senses, and appreciate your ability to do the task.

There is no doubt that your level of appreciation for the simple things in life is greatly deepened as soon as you are unable to do them. Being unable to walk gave me a far greater appreciation for the joy of walking through autumn leaves or along a wind-swept beach.

Next time you do the washing up, allow yourself to appreciate the hot soapy water so easily available to you; use your senses to smell the washing up liquid and to feel the frothy suds and the smooth, slippery plates. Make a conscious decision to enjoy the sensory experience rather than seeing it as a boring chore.

When was the last time you looked at something in nature? I'm not talking about a quick look through the window of a moving car or through your lounge window. I'm talking about looking as if through the eyes of a child or a Martian seeing Earth for the first time. Experiencing life fully, using all your senses, and tuning into nature's very essence and energy opens you up to a whole new world. The more you open yourself up to the experiences life offers, the greater the reward.

Most of us eat without any real attention, so we miss much of its potential pleasure. (It also contributes to weight gain as the 'I'm full' sensors in the brain are less likely to be triggered when we eat mindlessly.)

Try this simple exercise to experience what I mean. Buy a bar of really good quality chocolate. Choosing an unusual flavour can add to the experience. Set aside about ten minutes with no interruptions. First, look at the colour of the chocolate, and enjoy its aroma. Can you distinguish the ingredients from its smell? Take a pin or a cocktail stick, break off two squares of the chocolate, and eat the chocolate with the pin or stick, tiny morsel by tiny morsel. Allow the flavour to build upon your tongue as you slowly add more chocolate. Experiment by placing each pinfull on different parts of your tongue. What do you notice?

Few of us take the time to appreciate the amazing world we live in because the calls on our time and attention are many and various. Take the time to examine a flower or a single leaf. Look closely at the shape, colour, texture, and pattern. Can you identify the internal structure, the veining, for example? How does it feel? Does it have any smell? Is there any noise when you touch it–does it rustle?

Training yourself to experience things like this opens the way to appreciating life even more fully day to day. It leads to a greater sense of fulfilment.

Do What You Are Passionate About

How many of you are in a job that you don't enjoy, that doesn't give you any satisfaction? Or are you in a relationship that doesn't make you happy? Do you think this is all there is to life?

What are you passionate about? What makes you feel most excited and alive? How often do you get to experience the things which make you feel great?

Watch young children while they are playing and learning, and you will see they exude a sense of passion and joy. They have a natural curiosity about the world and how things work. They are ready to ask questions, to explore the endless possibilities, and to embrace life fully. Those who live a life of fulfilment and purpose enjoy a similar energy. They focus on the possibilities and see opportunities, which others less open to the experiences life has to offer, fail to recognise.

I recognise there are external pressures on adults to earn a living, to satisfy the expectations of others, and so on and so on. Nevertheless, despite all the pressures of modern-day living, finding true purpose and fulfilment are more about your state of mind and approach to life than the job and activities you do.

Are You Living Your Dream?

When you were young, what ambitions did you have? Did you have a dream to become a pilot, astronaut, artist, dancer, lawyer, or doctor? To write a bestseller or be a football player? Did you achieve your goal? If not, what got in the way? Was it simply a change of heart, or did others tell you that you were silly and needed to get real? Do you regret not living that early dream? Did you find a profession that makes you feel excited when you get up in the morning, do you feel indifferent or do you dread going to work?

I met a guy on a course a few years ago. He was a pilot on Concorde. He spoke of an upbringing where becoming a pilot was unthinkable. That all changed one day when he met someone who said to him, 'Someone has to pilot Concorde. Why shouldn't that someone be you?' From these words his perception of what was possible changed. He worked hard. Make no mistake, his journey was not straightforward, but he never gave up on his dream, and in time he succeeded.

I have worked with many clients who have had a life-changing illness or accident, or who have been made redundant. It is really common for those involved to see the situation as a real tragedy at the outset but to say later how it was the making of them. Their 'tragedy' provided the catalyst or gave them permission to do things very differently, and the result has been incredibly positive.

It seems a shame to wait until there is a potential disaster before you decide to give yourself the opportunity and the permission to shine. Sometimes you just have to take the risk and step into the unknown in order to gain a sense of purpose and fulfilment. It is important to explore those dreams again. Don't let others stomp on them.

What made you joyful as a child? Do you get to do it now? How do you spend your spare time now? Do your activities give you a sense of satisfaction, joy, and excitement? Are you still singing, playing sport, creating things–art, craft, cooking, photography, technology? Do you enjoy walking in beautiful places, gardening, experiencing nature, playing music, being with animals or birds, reading, or learning something new? What activities make you feel alive and energised? How often do you allow the time to immerse yourself in the things which fill you up and give you joy?

Do you have interests and hobbies, which add huge value to the quality of your life, or do you spend your time sitting in front of the TV or on social media? Reawakening old dreams or creating new ones is a great way of achieving a sense of purpose. Doing so can help you feel happy and fulfilled.

Don't be fooled into thinking that if you can't draw or paint, you are not creative. I use my garden to create an ever-changing environment. Being creative comes in many guises: poetry, writing, crafts, sewing, knitting, crochet, cooking, making music, photography, DIY building and repairs–the list is endless. Expanding yourself by exploring your creative side and stepping into your creativity offers enormous benefits to your sense of well-being, happiness, and fulfilment. The finished article is less important than the creative process, particularly when you start something new. Be adventurous and give lots of different things a try, until you find the right creative outlet for you.

Challenge Yourself

There is a qualitative difference between reacting to the challenges life brings and challenging yourself to be the best version of yourself. There is no doubt that we develop significantly as we deal with difficult situations. They offer us the opportunity to learn and grow, but there is a difference between reacting to what life throws at you and challenging yourself to be an even better version of you.

One of my challenges has been to recognise that being still and quiet is an important part of my development. It would have been all too easy to get caught up in the belief that my purpose was all about doing. One can get caught in the trap of constantly pursuing the illusion that purpose is all about achieving goals, each needing to be more important or profound than the ones before.

Living a Life with Passion

Living your passion and living with passion are entirely different things. Both are really important.

Living your passion is amazing. It makes work feel like playing. It is easy to get up in the morning as you know you are going to do something you love.

Living with passion means that you apply a sense of purpose and passion to everything you do. The activity doesn't matter half as much as the way you approach it. Doing the very best you can and doing it with enthusiasm and passion is what makes the real difference.

When I ran my school, every individual, whether a member of the senior management team, a teacher, a cleaner, or site manager, was seen as the leading professional for their area. They took the responsibility to do their job as well as possible with pride and passion. The result was a highly successful team, offering a great example to the children who attended. Of course, it may seem hard to be passionate about cleaning the toilets, but it is entirely possible when you see it as part of the bigger picture. Creating a clean and pleasant school environment was given high status by everyone.

No matter what you are doing, choose to do it with passion. Passion means you care and that you will not let anything get in your way. Passion is long-term, sustaining, deep-seated, and aligned with your inner core.

We Are All One! Being of Service

We are all connected. The decisions we make, the actions we take or fail to take, all have an impact on the people we know, the rest of mankind and on the world in which we live. Every act of kindness, however small, is significant. If the human race is to thrive, rather than simply survive, we must learn to enjoy our similarities and celebrate diversity. Many far more erudite people than I have captured the essence of unity and oneness and its importance.

Bonnie L. Oscarson said, 'We must stop concentrating on our differences and look for what we have in common. Then we can begin to realise our greatest potential and achieve the greatest good in the world'. Mother Teresa said, 'I can do things you cannot, you can do things I cannot; together we can do great things'. Bringing people together to share, model excellence, support and validate one another, and celebrate is vital if her aim is to be achieved. It is one of my motivations in creating the Thrive Together Tribe.

We live at a time when more people than ever are living on their own. People are living longer, and many people are lonely. Don't underestimate the positive impact you can make when you make contact with others. You have no idea what a difference a smile or a friendly word can make to a stranger. You may be the only person they have had contact with that day. Do you know your neighbours? How can you make a positive difference to people in your local or the wider community? An ancient African proverb recognises just how profound even the smallest act can be: "If you think you are too small to make a difference, you haven't spent the night with a mosquito."

The amazing thing about helping others is that you help yourself too. It will provide you with a tremendous sense of fulfilment.

People like Bob Geldof have the public profile and resources to create massive programmes such as Live Aid which can help many, but just as important are the small acts of service made individual by individual, day by day.

While getting involved in doing things for others could be seen as a one-way transaction, there is nothing further from the truth. You only have to see the huge pleasure and satisfaction millions of people get from being involved in raising money for many good causes like Children In Need or Comic Relief and helping out at homeless shelters, animal rescue centres, and community or conservation projects. They are gaining as much, if not more than those on the receiving end.

If you are feeling down or lonely, getting involved with a group that supports such projects is a great way to feel more fulfilled and to meet new people with like-minded interests. At the same time, you can take heart in the knowledge you are making a positive difference to others.

Random Acts of Kindness

One of the activities which can make a huge difference to the quality of your life and that of those around you is doing random acts of kindness–doing a kindness without any expectation of thanks or recognition.

Incorporating daily acts of random kindness has the power to create a sustained sense of positivity in even the most jaded of individuals. I have seen enormous differences in clients who were depressed, unhappy, or who felt they lacked direction and purpose, as a result of making random acts of kindness part of their daily routine. It can enhance your life if you are feeling good too. I know it has made an enormous difference to me.

It just takes a bit of thought and awareness of what is going on around you. It could be as simple as buying someone a cup of tea, helping someone carrying a heavy parcel, taking the washing in for a neighbour who is at work when it starts to rain heavily, offering to help a mum carry the push-chair up some steps, or phoning somebody that you know is lonely.

It doesn't have to cost a lot of time or money. It's just about looking for the opportunities and taking them when they present themselves. Be creative!

Most people find it quite easy to carry out random acts of kindness for others but have found a resistance to doing planned acts of kindness for themselves.

How can you nurture yourself? How can you be kind to yourself (kind rather than overindulgent)? Many clients have found this to be rather challenging initially, but well worth doing. If you don't know how to do that in the first instance, make a list of small things that you could do that make you feel good: giving yourself the luxury of taking a long leisurely bath, taking care of your hands and using hand cream, going to watch a film, or giving yourself time to read or meditate. Those random acts of kindness to yourself are about honouring and valuing yourself. This is incredibly important–YOU ARE WORTH IT.

Gratitude

Whilst this has been covered in detail earlier, it is important to remind you that gratitude is a vital component of feeling fulfilled. Being grateful becomes a way of being when you collect gratitudes on a daily basis. It re-calibrates the brain in the most positive way.

A Life Well-Lived

Bereavement is one of the most challenging things we have to deal with in life. Yet even in the pain of losing someone you love dearly, there are positive lessons if you choose to see them.

My much-loved younger brother, David, died quite unexpectedly and completely without warning. He was doing a final practice bicycle ride before the London to Brighton cycle race. Paradoxically, his chosen charity was the British Heart Foundation. During the ride, he appeared to fall off his bike. By the time he hit the road, he was dead. He had an undiagnosed congenital heart condition, which could have been easily rectified had it been identified.

In all the devastation and heartache there were clear lessons us all. His unexpected death urged us:

- To live every day as if it were our last
- To fully appreciate and nurture our relationships
- To love and laugh fully
- To confront our issues rather than be confrontational
- To let go of old hurts
- To do what we can to help others
- To leave the planet in better shape than it was when we arrived

I also urge you to look after your health and live a life with no regrets.

I was watching a TV programme recently that was following people who worked in hospices. Far from the miserable and sad atmosphere, you might expect, there was a sense of peace and contentment. Without exception, the staff talked about what an amazingly upbeat place hospices were. They described how the patients were determined to make the very best of every moment of what remained of their lives.

They spoke of how families and friends came together, how rifts were healed, and past hurts forgiven. I thought it sad that these families had to wait until the last moments of a loved one's life to deal with significant issues, which had gone on, sometimes for decades. My mum and dad taught us never to go to bed or leave the house on an argument. It has been a very wise principle. Happiness and fulfilment are so much more difficult to sustain if you are holding onto resentment or old hurts. I urge you to let go of the things which are getting in the way –to give yourself the gift of forgiveness, so you can forgive and heal the rift.

What Would You Like Your Legacy to Be?

Imagine yourself at your own funeral. What would you hear about yourself in the obituaries given by family, friends, and the wider community if you carry on living your life exactly as it is now?

Does it match what would you **wish** to hear others say about you, the life you have led, and the legacy you have left?

Ask yourself:

- Am I happy with my life?
- Do I love?
- Am I loved?
- Do I smile and laugh?
- Do I make others smile and laugh?
- Do I make a positive difference?
- Do I matter?
- Do I wish things were different?

It is absolutely your choice to continue as you are or to make some changes. You can choose to do whatever it takes to live your life in a way which makes your desired legacy a reality.

Faith

There is much written by far more qualified people than me about faith. I do not use the word faith attached to any specific formal religion or practice, but believe to live a life of purpose and fulfilment requires faith in self, others, the intrinsic goodness of life and a greater power than ourselves.

Wayne Dyer describes faith in one of his many articles about spirituality called, "Faith affirming," in the following words:

> *Faith is the complete reliance on the power and goodness of Spirit and the firm belief that you are always connected to this goodness. Always affirm*

your faith and not your doubt. When you affirm that things might not work out, that your troubles continue to mount, that your problems are insoluble, that God has not been listening, or that you are powerless in the face of so many struggles, you are affirming doubt rather than faith. The ability to know faith and affirm it allows it to manifest in your life.

In John 14:27, Jesus said, "My peace I give to you." This is an affirmation of faith. He certainly wasn't suggesting that peace is very difficult to have and you must struggle for it. Jesus brought peace to everyone by affirming it. Likewise, in his healing work, he didn't imply that we haven't been having a great deal of success lately with leprosy, but if you listen to me you have a thirty percent chance of surviving over the next five years. Instead, he declared, "You are well," affirming faith at the highest spiritual level, and healing took place.

You too must learn to affirm your faith in the face of doubt with thoughts that things will work out, things will improve. Think, write, and say affirmations like these:

I intend to create prosperity.

I'll do what is necessary to eradicate this problem.

I know I am not alone.

I have faith that all is for good.

I give no energy to the negative because I know all is in divine order.

I will consult with God and know that I will be guided to do what is needed.

These are all affirmations of faith, which, when practised, will permit you to say "no" to doubt and "yes" to life.

Wayne Dyer chose an example of faith from the Bible, but it is important to recognise that every world religion has faith at its core. Faith is a very personal thing. It has the capacity to engender incredibly strong emotions. Over the centuries many wars have been fought in the name of rival faiths with both sides convinced they were right and that they had God on their side.

I have faith there will come a time when we can all live in harmony, celebrating our differences as well as our similarities. I doubt it will come in my lifetime, but I'm hopeful that there is a growing body of people who believe it is not only vital, but that it is possible, and they are doing their best to facilitate the change. I see myself as one of them and hope you do too. If this beautiful planet we call home is to have any chance of surviving, the human race has to learn to live very differently. Protecting the natural world and recognising how important it is to conserve, share, and collaborate have to become a way of life.

I hope that Secret Pathway 5 has given you food for thought, and expanded your sense of self, so you see yourself as a spiritual being, rather than someone who simply spends their life frantically trying to complete their to-do list and please everyone who makes demands on you. It is important that you appreciate that you ARE enough, just as you are. That you recognise the quality of your life will be very different if you live in the moment and when you take the time to be. That you realise when you live your passion in life and live your life with passion, life takes on a joyful quality which is missing when you don't. It is never too late to find your passion; the important thing is to give yourself permission to explore and experiment until you do.

So what now? How will you move things forward? Which of the ideas, principles, and strategies will you use to make a positive difference in your life? Remember, if you always do what you have always done, you will always get what you have already. If you are happy, successful, and feel truly fulfilled just as you are, congratulations! However, if you believe your life could be even better, it is worth incorporating the tools and ways of being I have shared with you here.

Chapter 9

This Is Not The End

Today is the beginning of the rest of your life. You cannot change what has happened in the past, but you can change the way you deal with the aftermath of that past. You can choose to let go of past hurts and forgive, allowing yourself to move on and enjoy the freedom it brings. None of us knows what the future holds, and worrying about it does nothing to change the outcome.

All we have is the present moment–the now. It is your choice whether your life will continue in the same old way because you do nothing differently, or you can enhance the quality of your life and that of those around you by incorporating some or all of the strategies and ways of thinking that were shared in the Underpinning Principles, Connecting Themes, and Secret Pathways.

Awareness is only the first step; it is vital, but without sustained action, nothing will change in the long term. Give yourself permission to do what it takes to create a life full of happiness, success and fulfilment.

A shift in perspective or a change of focus has the capacity to change things significantly, but it requires you to be open to a world of different possibilities.

It is your choice whether fear or love runs your life. Remember, the main difference between highly successful people and those who get no further than wishing they were successful is not that highly successful people feel no fear. It is that they feel the fear and get on with what needs to be done despite the fear.

Forgiveness is not about forgetting or condoning, but it is about letting go of the negative aspects of your past so that you can enjoy a different quality of life–understanding that, has helped many clients find freedom from the trauma and hurt inflicted on them. It has the capacity to help you to do the same.

Learning the amazing power of gratitude and incorporating a daily act of gratitude can be transformational; it is so easy to do, it installs a more positive way of looking at the world, and it costs nothing.

Allowing yourself to be more playful, to be curious, and to see the world as an exciting place where anything is possible, will give you more opportunities to smile and to laugh. Learning to be childlike rather than childish is an important element of being playful.

Becoming aware of the way in which you think, being mindful rather than staying stuck in the mire of habitual patterns of thinking, speaking, and acting has the capacity to transform your life and those around you, but it takes practice.

It is your choice whether you spend your time complaining, feeling fearful, and focusing on what you lack, or focusing on the great things in your life and the things you can do. Taking total responsibility for your own emotional wellbeing is a giant step towards achieving ongoing happiness, success, and fulfilment; by doing so, you are no longer dependent on other's moods or actions. You take control of your life.

Believing in yourself and your ability, having faith that you ARE enough is a vital step towards true fulfilment. Developing the confidence to share your vulnerability with others and to ask for what you want, in an upfront straightforward way without complaining or seeing yourself as a victim is a strength, one which can be learned.

The old disempowering beliefs which have held you back could be a thing of the past if you take on board the essence of Secret Pathway 1.

Holding beliefs which support your confidence and self-worth is paramount if you want to be happy and successful, or be able to create loving, interdependent relationships. Your beliefs determine whether you will succeed or fail in love, financially, at work, and in life. They impact on how effectively you deal with the challenges life throws at you. They govern how well you deal with stress and anxiety. Your beliefs affect how happy, successful, and prosperous you will be, and the level of abundance you will experience throughout your life. Given how powerful they are, it is vital that you ensure you have beliefs that underpin your success, happiness and fulfilment rather than allow any beliefs that limit you to remain unchecked.

Learning to love who you are is the first vital step towards creating lasting, loving, successful relationships with others. All the principles and practical strategies shared in Secret Pathway 2 are designed to help you achieve a positive, loving relationship with yourself. Doing so will make a qualitative difference to your personal and professional relationships. It also gives you the very best chance of creating and sustaining a great relationship with your partner.

Incorporating the strategies of highly successful people outlined in Secret Pathway 3 can help you achieve even greater success. Modelling those who have mastery of anything is a great way of short-circuiting the learning process. Why make heavy weather of it, if others have trodden the route before and can show you the shortcuts and help you avoid the hazards?

Secret Pathway 4 puts you firmly in the driver's seat. Life consists of a huge range of choices, transitions and changes. We can be assured that each stage will bring its own unique challenges. Those who embrace change and see it as a natural part of daily life will find that life is much more comfortable. Everything you do or say is your choice and responsibility. As soon as you choose to take control of your life, navigation becomes easier, no matter how challenging the journey may be.

Understanding what motivates you and others has made a huge difference in my life and that of the many people I've shared it with. Whether you are dealing with other family members, friends, clients, your colleagues, or your boss, this model can help you too.

Identifying your true purpose can feel elusive, but by giving yourself space and learning to enjoy the silence will give you the best chance to engage your intuition. Learning to be a human being rather than a human doing can feel out of reach, but remember it's a process, not a competition. Those who know their purpose have a head start, it is not a race, remember the story of the hair and the tortoise. It's not about how quickly you can discover your purpose, but what you do with it once you have discovered it which brings total fulfilment.

You deserve to live a happy, successful and abundant life, full of joy and fulfilment. Each of the elements within *Thriving Not Surviving* is designed to help you achieve such a life.

The Thrive Together Tribe

So what now? I've shared with you some principles and strategies which have the capacity to make a qualitative difference to the quality of your life, but if they stay as words on the pages, there will be little that will change. It is only when you choose to incorporate some of them into your life that they have the opportunity to work.

Research has shown unequivocally that people who are surrounded by a positive peer group when they are trying to implement change have a far better chance of success, than those who try it alone. Things are even more successful when those peers provide support, challenge, encouragement, and accountability.

If you want lasting transformation, it is important to have someone in your corner to help you: witnessing your intentions, providing the right sort of help and support, holding you accountable, and celebrating your successes with you. Because the impact of having such a support group is so instrumental in helping create and maintain lasting change, as mentioned in the introduction, I have created just such a support group called the Thrive Together Tribe. It is an online membership group, which offers a positive peer group, ongoing support, access to a bank of further information, and strategies to help you on your journey. To learn more and join the group go to: www.thrivetogethertribe.com. In the future, I hope to hold Thrive Together Tribe meetings where members can meet in person to share and learn.

I know the principles and strategies really work when used consistently. The Thrive Together Tribe is designed to help you maintain your focus, so you could achieve your goals more easily. You can tap into the ongoing support that belonging to our tribe offers through the regular themed presentations, interactive sessions, the ongoing discussion forum, access to the ever-growing resource bank of information, guest speakers, and advice. Being part of our tribe means you will have active supporters who believe in the power of YOU even when you are struggling to believe it yourself.

The Thrive Together Tribe provides an opportunity to communicate with others who are going through the same challenges as you and those who have successfully moved beyond them. Creative juices often flow best when discussions take place. Ideas come out of sharing and exploring with others.

It is really tricky negotiating your way through life's trials and tribulations, and doing it on your own makes it feel much harder. Many of my clients say they don't want to burden their close family and friends, or they fear they will be judged negatively. Knowing they can feel safe to share their innermost fears and issues in a non-judgemental and supportive environment makes them feel more confident and empowered.

Being seen, heard, and validated are central pillars of the Thrive Together Tribe. There will always be someone on hand to offer a listening ear, support, and advice, or to simply hold the space for you. How would it feel to know that there is someone who truly cares about you? To feel you belong, that you matter and that you can succeed and contribute to the success of others?

Today is the beginning of the rest of your life. You can't change the past, but you sure as hell can change your present and your future. The Thrive Together Tribe offers the insights, challenges, and support to help you understand your life purpose and achieve lasting fulfilment whilst you are on the most amazing journey called life.

One of the most powerful antidotes dealing with your most challenging issues is to feel part of a group where you know you matter. That is the role of the Thrive Together Tribe. I have created it for people who want to belong to something which recognises them as individuals: a safe place to feel heard and seen, one where you will be valued for the amazing person you are when you are being genuinely you. A forum to raise questions and issues, and be offered support and advice, and a platform to celebrate your wins and successes. A place to belong! The Thrive Together Tribe is for those who want to get the very best out of life. It is a place where you can be nurtured, supported, heard, and seen by like-minded people, people who have made the choice to be happy, successful and fulfilled. You can dip in and visit whenever you have the need to take a breath, step off the world, relax, and be you. To learn more, join us at www.thrivetogethertribe.com

I hope you will join me and become part of the group of people who are determined to thrive–together.

Lightning Source UK Ltd.
Milton Keynes UK
UKHW021221140120
356930UK00005B/304/P

9 781641 363617